21 YEARS OF SHARJAH INTERNATIONAL CR...

HOWZAT!

BY PHILIP MOORE

IN MEMORY OF GEOFF MOORE WHO KNEW MORE ABOUT
THE GAME THAN ANYONE I'VE KNOWN

WITH THANKS

A number of people have assisted, advised or contributed to the compilation of this book. In no particularly order, the author wishes to thank: AR Bukhatir, John McDonald, John Nowell, Nick Crawley and all at Zodiac Publishing, Qasim Noorani, and the late Geoff Moore. Special thanks to Khaleej Times chief librarian Aziz Rehman and his colleague, C Aboobakar. They were never too busy to look up a score or track down an old photo or cutting. But then there's something about those yellowing files that only hacks, and those who file their copy, truly understand.

Photographs in this book have been supplied by Touchline, AllSport, Jorge Ferrari, Khaleej Times, Gulf News and Philip Moore

Special thanks for the corporate support to Iain Everingham, Mazhar-ud-Deen, Naresh Bhatia and Jan Yorke of Shell Markets (Middle East) Limited, not only for their support of my book but also for their ongoing support of cricket; It was a pleasure to have Steve Burd and Bryan Moulds of TNT providing invaluable back up and distribution; Burjor Patel of Khaleej Times and I also appreciated the support of Sharjah Commerce & Tourism Development Authority.

HOWZAT!
21 YEARS OF SHARJAH INTERNATIONAL CRICKET

Published by Zodiac Publishing.

Zodiac Publishing, USA
#4 Herndon House, Canon Creek Air Park,
Rt. 18, P.O.Box 589, Lake City,
Florida 32025, USA.
Tel: 386 754 6527
e-mail: zodiacpublishing@hotmail.com

Zodiac Publishing, UK.
#3 Carlyle Court, Chelsea Harbour,
London SW10 0UQ, UK.
Tel: 020 7352 8910 Fax: 020 7376 4271
e-mail: zodiacpublishing@hotmail.com

Zodiac Publishing, FZ LLC, UAE.
#302 Dubai Media City,
P.O.Box 35121, Dubai, UAE
Tel: 0971 4 - 2826966 Fax: 0971 4 - 2826882
e-mail: zodiacp@emirates.net.ae

First published 2002

Copyright: Philip Moore 2002

ISBN 0 - 9721589-9-5

British Library Cataloguing - in - Publication Data.
A catalogue record for this book is available
from the British Library.

Design by Nick Crawley of Zodiac Publishing.
Separations & Printing by Emirates Printing Press, Dubai.

CONTENTS

CHAPTER 1

FIRST PAGE OF THE FAIRYTALE

A young Arab student in Pakistan burned the midnight oil listening to BBC broadcasts of Test cricket from far-flung lands. His heroes had names like Hanif, Pataudi, Benaud, May and Worrell.

Abdulrahman Bukhatir returned to the United Arab Emirates (UAE) and presided over a multi-million dollar empire, mainly in banking, building and construction. But the radio remained tuned to the Tests.

In the shadows of the great mosques of the Gulf where the faithful are called to prayer, expatriates played this foreign game with the gusto, if not the skill, of their idols in the respective nations they called home. Matches were played at the Royal Air Force base in Sharjah in the pre-oil boom 1950s. In 1974, the young businessman and useful all-rounder (he captained his school team in Karachi) formed the local Bukhatir League.

International teams - mainly sponsored sides from India and Pakistan - started filtering through to the Gulf, thanks to the enthusiasm of Bukhatir. In 1977 more than 3,000 fans gathered for a match between a Pakistan International Airlines team and players based locally. The Ruler of Sharjah, HH Sheikh Sultan bin Mohammed Al Qasimi, came to watch. The pitch was a strip of cement, the outfield grassless and flint-hard. But it was a game of cricket and everyone who turned up loved every minute.

Response to any imported team, particularly sides from the subcontinent, was always highly enthusiastic. Double-wicket competitions featuring the likes of Ian Botham and Clive Lloyd came later.

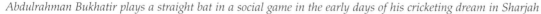

Abdulrahman Bukhatir plays a straight bat in a social game in the early days of his cricketing dream in Sharjah

Bukhatir would have taken on Napoleon if it helped bring fully-fledged international cricket to his hometown. More than that, he'd have bowled to Bradman all day on concrete or faced Larwood without a helmet.

In a wide-ranging interview in 1984 the reserved but always accessible Bukhatir said of the development of his fondness for the game: "I was 12 years old and the only Arab in the class. Cricket was by far the most popular game and there was just no way I could refuse to join in, basically because everyone else played.

"I was not what you would call a 'born cricketer', but I managed to get a feel for the game and understand its finer points. There are so many aspects to cricket. It has a much wider scope than any other game that I know."

Bukhatir is a traditionalist when it comes to cricket. He knows the game inside and out. He delights in its lore. The traditional cradle of cricket is what gave birth to the soaraway Sharjah success.

Bukhatir's business empire flourished and, in 1980, the ultimate fan built a stadium - totally from his personal funds - to develop international cricket in the emirate. Bukhatir was known as a great fielder, never missing a catch, few believed the esoteric sport would take root, let alone blossom, in the desert sands.

"I was really chasing a childhood dream all those years," Bukhatir noted. "I used to worship the big names of cricket, like Hanif Mohammed. When I returned to Sharjah I didn't even play for a long time, but I wanted so much to promote the game here that I started playing again, to set an example."

In doing so he ran the gauntlet of more than a few caustic comments from curious Arab friends bewildered by his enthusiasm for this odd and complex sport. Some big-name players had been to the region, true, but generally, cricketers around the world knew far less about Sharjah than Sharjah knew about cricket.

Now, of course, Sharjah is the leading One Day International venue in the world. Twenty-one extraordinary years have passed since a sell-out crowd packed the little ground for Sharjah's first international between teams from India and Pakistan. It has even staged two Test matches.

It is typical of Bukhatir's nature that he went ahead with fulfilling his dream, not to benefit himself but the cricketers he idolised. He spent heavily setting up

international series. Profits went to a benefit fund for top players, in tribute to his boyhood passion. The Cricketers Benefit Fund Series (CBFS) - the convener of matches at the 'desert oasis' - designates former players as financial beneficiaries of tournaments.

Bukhatir said: "When PIA (Pakistan International Airlines) brought a team over with players like Majid Khan, Imran Khan and Mudassar Nazar, we played them at the old ground and were surprised by the number of people who turned out to watch. Everything else just followed naturally. With a benefit match in mind, we started out by building a green surface and a pavilion.

"The first year was just with temporary stands erected out of building scaffolding. Again we had a full house and we were worried that the scaffolding might collapse. Immediately after that we thought, 'Why not build a proper stadium?' And we did."

Players past and present laud the CBFS and its salutary activities. Barry Richards, the great South African opening batsman, told the author: "Sharjah provides great help to players, particularly from the subcontinent. Some of the older players who might not be as well known and might not have done as well financially, have been assisted. "

Ravi Shastri, the champion Indian all-rounder, added: "Bukhatir was a visionary. I consider myself privileged to have played in those early games in Sharjah. You knew something very special was happening."

And so many Indians and Pakistanis, backbone of the workforce in the UAE, shared Bukhatir's passion. They embraced the first international match in 1981 and continue to ensure all major contests are sell-out affairs.

Within three years Sharjah lured a team from England, the nation that appears to have evolved the game from about the year 1300 and whose Oliver Cromwell had 'indulged' it as far back as 1640.

Apart from Bukhatir, the most outstanding contribution to the Sharjah experiment has been by Qassim Noorani. Their friendship dates back to Bukhatir's school days; their love for cricket, further still. A serene and stylish character, Noorani came to the UAE in the early 1970s to assist Bukhatir in his business. International cricket may have been a long way off, but, if Bukhatir had the dream and the drive, Noorani possessed the organisational skills. It made for a great opening combination.

"So many people scoffed at the idea of cricket being played at the top level here in Sharjah – but now Sharjah is part of world cricket, simple as that," says Noorani.

Sharjah has built a reputation for far more than attractive prize money. Teams have come to appreciate its non-partisan character, given the policy of neutral umpires and the absence on most occasions of a national UAE team. Neutral umpiring was pioneered in Sharjah and is now accepted worldwide.

Since the inception of international cricket in Sharjah the inevitable comparisons have been made between Bukhatir and Kerry Packer, the Australian media tycoon who set up his own World Series 'Circus.' For years Bukhatir's stock reply was: "Kerry Packer makes money from cricket – I don't." Nowadays Bukhatir probably makes money out of the Sharjah success, but it would be negligible to what would be on offer if he invested the same sums elsewhere. "It is my most expensive hobby," he is fond of saying.

Strolling across the Sharjah ground's outfield with Bukhatir at the conclusion of yet another successful tournament is to witness a man clearly happy with his lot. Sharjah has hosted more one-day cricket internationals (181) than any other venue in the world since CBFS commenced operations in 1981.

It is difficult to define the Golden Age of any sport, but it seems the early- and mid-1980s are deemed a halcyon period for Sharjah. Ravi Shastri feels some of the matches were "among the greatest limited over games ever played."

Bukhatir acknowledges this, but is hard-pressed to pinpoint the most magical moment that occurred or match played on his field of dreams. He acknowledges, of course, Javed Miandad's last-ball six to beat India, scrambling wins by Australia and England over each other, the toss of the coin for the first international fixture, and so much more.

He pauses for a moment before citing a delightful incident that only a cricketer could love - the Australians scurrying from the field during an uncustomary Sharjah cloudburst.

"It felt like... like cricket," he says.

Just as it did when the broadcasts crackled through the radio speaker in Karachi when it all started – A.R Bukhatir's endless summer.

How the game has changed... South Africa's Ntini sends West Indies Brian Lara on his way

CHAPTER 2

ASIF IQBAL: FROM PACKER TO BUKHATIR

Asif Iqbal played a role just as cavalier, charming and prominent, in organising the Sharjah tournaments as the all-rounder did in his distinguished playing days. Indeed, Asif Iqbal Razvi, who shared the Bukhatir dream for more than two decades, coined the expression 'Offshore Cricket.'

The former Hyderabad, Karachi, Kent, Pakistan and World XI player was responsible for so much of the careful planning and imaginative thinking that took the Sharjah experiment to the exalted position of number one limited-over cricket venue in the world. He was co-ordinator of the CBFS from the outset.

Asif, the nephew of Ghulam Ahmed, the Indian spinner, was a stylish batsman, particularly quick on his feet and strong on the leg side. He loved to attack the ball and the tougher the conditions the better he seemed to like it. He was brought up in Hyderabad in Southern India and played for Hyderabad in the Ranji Trophy from 1959 before emigrating to Pakistan in 1961.

His Test debut for Pakistan was in 1964/5 against Australia. He batted at number 10 (scoring 41 and 36) and formed an unlikely bowling partnership with Majid Khan. Both, of course, were to become much better known for their batting acumen. Asif, however, remained a sound second-tier seamer for his entire career.

By 1967, on a tour of England, his class as a batsman was really starting to show. He went in at number nine in the Lord's Test, scoring 76 in a stand of 130 with the great Hanif Mohammad. It was a record for Pakistan for the eighth wicket. Then came the Test at the Oval when the Pakistanis were 65 for the loss of eight wickets in their second innings – and still 159 behind England. Asif shared a wonderful stand of 190 in 175 minutes with Intikhab Alam for the ninth wicket. Asif scored 146, including two sixes and 21 fours. In the first innings he had taken the new ball and snared three for 66 in 42 overs.

He joined Kent in 1968 and served the county with distinction, scoring more than 1,000 runs in a season on six occasions. His greatest Test season was 1976/7 when he hit four centuries in three different series. Touring Australia that season he made 313 runs in three tests (at 78.25), including 152 not out at the Adelaide Oval and 120 at the Sydney Cricket Ground in the third of the three-Test series when Pakistan beat Australia away from home for the first time.

Sitting in the stands at Sharjah and reminiscing, Asif feels that the centuries in Australia, facing Dennis Lillee at his fiercest and finest, were his best knocks, along with a brave 135 in Kingston a few months later against a West Indies' attack spearheaded by Andy Roberts.

Ever the stylist, Asif was distinguished, however, by an unusual cross-handed grip. The left hand held the bottom of the bat, the right hand was on top. Whatever, his extraordinary speed of eye and footwork ensured that no so-called technical deficiency

Asif Iqbal... Sharjah pioneer

would ever be a setback.

"I often wonder," Asif told the author, "if I would have had any career at all if coaches had changed my grip. It worked for me and that should be the main thing when it comes to coaching. People should play with flair and however they feel comfortable."

Asif Iqbal was at the forefront of the fight for better pay for Pakistan's top players as well as a leading light in Kerry Packer's World Series Cricket.

"I consider myself to be so fortunate to have had the opportunity to work for Kerry Packer and Abdulrahman Bukhatir," he said. "Initially, we had not heard of this extraordinary man Bukhatir, or his dream. What he did is nothing short of remarkable."

In the early 1980s rumours abounded that Kerry Packer would visit Sharjah. Some even said he had already been. Certainly some high-ranking Packer lieutenants dropped in from time to time. But there was always speculation Packer himself slipped in incognito, wearing everything from a *ghutra* to dark glasses.

"No," said Asif. "He didn't come . . . he definitely didn't come."

Asif Iqbal left the Sharjah scene when the sport was turned upside down. But his contribution to the Sharjah experiment remains immense.

The Sharjah icon's association with the CBFS came to an abrupt end in April, 2001. It followed the decision of the Indian Government not to allow the national squad to play at "non-regular" venues such Sharjah, Toronto and Singapore. The withdrawal came only two weeks from the start of a Sharjah tournament scheduled to feature India, Pakistan and Sri Lanka.

Asif said: "I am used to dealing with only cricket and cricket boards. I am not ready to deal with people who have nothing to do with cricket."

Bukhatir said he was sorry to see him go and added: " Asif's resignation was a personal decision, but we have worked together for 20 years. Hence, we cannot forget him. "

CHAPTER 3

BATSMEN READY . . . ?
RIGHT ARM OVER . . . .

April 3, 1981: two of the all-time greats, Sunil Gavaskar and Javed Miandad, lead their respective sides - named in their honour - on to the green, green grass of Sharjah stadium.

More than 8,000 fans have jammed the arena. 'Offshore Cricket', is clearly going to make an impact on the game in a most emphatic manner.

"First up, we were concerned not many people would come, but then the queues outside the ground stretched so far and so many people started taking up their positions that I really did fear the scaffolding we'd erected for seating might collapse," Asif Iqbal recalls.

For the record, Gavaskar won the toss and elected to bat.

The Gavaskar XI scored 139 for the loss of eight wickets in the allotted 45 overs. The Miandad XI overtook it in 32.5 overs for the loss of only three wickets.

It was talked about as a feast of cricket and so it transpired. None of the stars 'cried off', each wanting to be part of the special Sharjah 'something.' Gavaskar, Vengsarkar and Kapil Dev were household names and they had actually come to Sharjah. Gavaskar's XI also contained a gangling young left-arm orthodox spinner and lower-order batsman destined for greatness. His name was Ravi Shastri.

Pakistan's best had also caught the plane to the UAE, including the 'Lion of Lahore', Imran Khan. The elegant Zaheer Abbas, Wasim Raja and Mudassar Nazar - it was a purist's delight and an autograph hunter's dream. The superstars of the subcontinent were mobbed at every opportunity.

The match was played in honour of two former Pakistan skippers, Asif Iqbal and the legendary Hanif Mohammed. The two main beneficiaries received $50,000 each. Hanif at that stage held the record for the highest individual score in first-class cricket, 499. It has since been bettered by West Indian Brian Lara's 501.

History now records that the first two batsmen to walk on to Sharjah Stadium in an international were Gavaskar and Chetan Chauhan. Pakistan's new-ball pair was Sikandar Bakht and the hostile young speedster Imran Khan.

Pakistan put the brakes on early. India could manage only nine runs in the first five overs. Then Asif

Iqbal, delighted to be a beneficiary in this historic game, was brought into the attack by Miandad. Gavaskar welcomed him in the time-honoured fashion, with two murderous cuts to the boundary. The man they called 'the Bombay Bradman' showed why he deserved the nickname that was a headline writer's dream.

Both openers started to score more freely. Miandad

Kapil Dev, India's official Cricketer of the Century leads the charge in Sharjah

11

Ravi Shastri, the champion Indian all-rounder, first came to the UAE as a player but is now a regular commentator

turned to Iqbal Qasim and was rewarded with two quick wickets. The left-arm spinner tempted Chauhan to have a swing and Taslim Arif completed a tidy stumping. Qasim then sent off Vengsarkar for a duck, with Taslim again lending a hand, this time with a sharp catch.

Sandeep Patil and Gavaskar kept the scoreboard ticking over with some well-judged singles, but the line and length of Qasim and Mudassar made boundaries hard to come by. The important wicket of Gavaskar came when the little opener was on 37. He was over-ambitious with a drive off Mudassar and holed out to Imran.

Kirti Azad thumped four boundaries in quick succession before being given a life when Miandad dropped a skier of Sikandar's bowling. Azad was soon out for 20 to Sikandar with Miandad holding the catch.

The free-flowing Patil tried to bolster the run rate, but Imran, back for a second spell, was in full cry. Patil found the edge as he tried to turn a particularly quick ball from Imran down the leg side. Taslim took a sharp chance to end Patil's handy innings at 33.

Although the Indian players didn't look likely to compile a big score, Pakistan couldn't breathe easier until the greatest obstacle, Kapil Dev, was out of the way. The hard-hitting middle-order batsman was run out for one and the appeal could just about be heard in the adjacent emirate of Dubai, 20 minutes' drive down what was then a single-lane road.

Pakistan's bowling had simply been too tidy and tight for Gavaskar's team on the day. Qasim bowled four maidens in his nine-over quota during which he picked up two wickets and conceded only 19 runs. Imran (9-1-20-2), rated one of the world's best fast bowlers, gave the crowd the chance to witness what all the fuss was about.

Chasing such a small target, the Miandad XI bats-

men ensured they wouldn't get bogged down! Opener Sadiq Mohammed, a veteran who cut his teeth on Dennis Lillee, timed the ball superbly. His innings will be remembered especially for a magnificent cover drive for four off Kapil in the second over as well as his onslaught on young Shastri. Sadiq twice hammered Shastri for sixes over midwicket.

Taslim Arif, who 'kept so well, carried on the good form with the bat. He was particularly severe on Kapil and Yograj Singh. No bowler could induce a false shot from either opener and it seemed the only way they were likely to be dismissed would be through run-outs.

Sadiq attempted a risky single for the 50 he richly deserved. Azad rifled in a return and Reddy did the necessaries. Sadiq's 49 included two sixes and four fours. The century partnership with Taslim took only 21 overs, which was all the more noteworthy because of the slow outfield.

Miandad took strike to a thunderous ovation, but was out for two. He tried to guide Ghavri to the vacant slip and instead edged the ball to Reddy. Taslim, who was in regal form, was gone four runs later for 53 when another wonderful throw from Azad shattered the stumps at the bowler's end.

In the space of three overs and eight runs Pakistan saw three of the top order back in the dressing room. But it was only a hiccup as Zaheer (21) and Wasim Raja (12) saw the team home without further incident. Zaheer hit three fours and, for good measure, drove Yadav for a massive six.

The roll of honour of those who have won man-of-the-match awards at Sharjah is the veritable who's who of the game. However, the first recipient was Taslim Arif, whose stumping, catching and batting skills ensured the first international match at Sharjah Stadium would be won by the Miandad XI of Pakistan.

The winning Miandad XI picked up $15,000 while Gavaskar's team pocketed $5,000.

Gavaskar said: "I was proud to be associated with this game."

Miandad's verdict: "I'm thrilled. The occasion has been a roaring success."

Cricket's seed had been planted in the desert. The international circuit would never be the same again.

CHAPTER 4

THE BOYS ARE BACK IN TOWN

April now meant cricket at Sharjah Stadium. Offshore cricket had proved its point in 1981 and was back in 1982, again featuring elite players from India and Pakistan.

There were two scheduled matches at this carnival. Sunil Gavaskar again skippered the Indian team while captaincy duties for the Pakistan line-up went to the crafty spinner, Intikhab Alam.

The matches were for the benefit of Gavaskar and Intikhab. Sponsors Rothmans donated a rolling trophy and $40,000 in prize-money was on offer. Adding to the festivities of the CBFS International Week was the Bukhatir International Double-Wicket Competition in which four international and two UAE pairs took part.

The Gavaskar XI won the first match in 41.3 overs and in fine style before 7,000 spectators. Many others couldn't get in.

Test stars Dilip Doshi and Madanlal bowled the Gavaskar side to the 15-run victory after some fine batting by Shastri, Yashpal Sharma and Patil. Yet the Indian team got off to the worst possible start when Gavaskar was brilliantly caught by Imran Khan at deep fine leg off the bowling of fellow paceman Tahir Naqqash.

Shastri, the other opener, adopted a sheet-anchor role while Sharma cut loose. Sharma's quick-fire 64 included two huge sixes and four fours. He was eventually well caught by Saleem Malik - 18 years away from a life ban - off the bowling of the ever-reliable Nazar. Patil carried on Sharma's good work and belted two sixes of his own in a 43-minute score of 47 before falling to Naqqash. The composed Shastri was run out for 69, but a big total looked on the cards, especially with Kapil likely to cut loose.

Then Imran unleashed one of the fiercest spells of bowling imaginable. Imran had gone wicketless in his first spell, but made up for it when he returned to destroy the Indian middle order. His four wickets, Kapil (9), Azad, (6), Madanlal (0) and Kirmani (7) were all bowled middle stump. Pakistan finished on a high, but the marvellous 113 second-wicket partnership between Shastri and Sharma was the cornerstone of the eight for 210 total.

Muddassar and Mohsin, two of the best openers in the world, got Intikhab's team off to a breezy start, but

Imran Khan... lethal with bat or ball

Madanlal got a good ball through the defence of Mudassar (20) who was adjudged lbw. Mohsin and Miandad were involved in an horrendous mix-up with both players stranded at one end. Miandad, Pakistan's leading run scorer of all time, was out for four.

Zaheer and Raja steadied the ship before left-arm spinner Dilip Doshi produced a sparkling spell that claimed Zaheer (24), Raja (17), Imran (23) and Haroon (7). Pakistan regrouped and gave chase. Intikhab got stuck into Doshi, hitting him for two sixes in the same over. Shastri too suffered at the hands of Intikhab and Malik, who hit him for a huge six. Pakistan inched closer.

Gavaskar called on Madanlal to finish off the Pakistanis and he duly obliged. The tall and talented opening bowler took the wickets of Malik (19), Arif (4) and Naqqash (0). The match ended with the Intikhab XI all out for 210 after a spectacular stumping of Naqqash by Kirmani off the bowling of the speedy Madanlal.

The return clash for the Rothmans Trophy seven days later looked likely to again go the way of the in-form Indian team. Gavaskar won the toss and asked Intikhab's men to bat. The decision yielded quick results as Mohsin went first ball when Shastri took a neat catch after a great ball from Madanlal. Zaheer was run out for 14 and Miandad, who hit a six and looked threatening, played a lazy shot against Shastri and 'keeper Kirmani held the catch.

Mudassar, who had been watching all of this from the other end, kept his head down and ground out the first century (115) in an international competition at Sharjah. But Pakistan needed quick runs down the order and Imran supplied some of them with 46 while Wasim Raja hit a brisk 35. The Pakistanis scored a more-than-useful four for 240 off 45 overs.

Pakistan took to the field to defend the total and Imran worked up blistering pace. He sent Gavaskar packing for 11, caught Taslim.

Vishwanath (35), Patil (74) and Kapil (41) ensured the Indian team was always within striking distance. Patil played some dashing strokes and Kapil middled the ball and his innings had that 'anything can happen' look. Indeed, the fifth-wicket partnership between Patil and Kapil yielded 95. Imran's re-introduction put paid to any thoughts of a win by the Gavaskar XI, especially when a scorcher trapped Kapil lbw. Imran tore through the tail and, after 42.3 overs the Gavaskar XI was out for 196, well short of the total. The teams had won a game each, but the silverware went to Intikhab's side on superior run-rate. Imran shaded Mudassar for man-of-the-match honours.

CHAPTER 5

EVERYONE'S A WINNER

The Sharjah cricket experiment had been 'playing itself in' during the tournaments of 1981 and 1982. It came of age in March 1983 when England played Pakistan in a match approved by the Board of Control for Cricket in Pakistan and the English Test and County Cricket Board. High-ranking cricket authorities from Lords and the BCCP as well as India's Board of Control would run an eye over the event. Major CBFS beneficiaries were the fine Pakistani batsman Zaheer Abbas, who had just completed a century of centuries in First Class cricket, and Indian star Gundappa Vishwanath. Both would receive $50,000.

Skipper Bob Willis pulled out at the last minute, but England arrived in the UAE with a side hardened in a tough Ashes campaign they lost 2-1 to Australia. David Gower, one of the most gifted batsmen in the world, captained a team to Sharjah that included Allan Lamb, Geoff Cook, Bob Taylor and the awesome Ian Botham.

Meanwhile, Imran Khan led one of Pakistan's finest-ever sides. It boasted the likes of Mudassar Nazar, Mohsin Khan, Zaheer, Wasim Raja and the ultimate competitor, Javed Miandad.

Adding spice to the contest was a debate raging throughout the cricket world over who was the greater all-rounder out of Imran, Botham, Kapil Dev or Richard, later Sir Richard Hadlee. Botham told the author – in no uncertain manner – that the others were well short of being able to lay claim to his unofficial title.

There was $40,000 prize money on offer to the teams plus extra for individual awards, but the high costs of bringing the international game to Sharjah were not passed on to the eager fans. Indeed, the CBFS discussed rates of admission and actually lowered the price to ensure anyone wishing to see the spectacular showcase would not be disappointed. Admission rates were: 150 dirhams (players pavilion), 150 dirhams (covered stand A), 50 dirhams (covered enclosure) and 25 dirhams (general).

Pakistan's victory came in the 43rd over when Imran blasted Norman Cowans for a six into the back of the stands. England scored nine for 218 in their allotted 45 overs with opener Graeme 'Foxy' Fowler defying the best of Imran's pace and Abdul Qadir's spin to score 108 in 154 minutes. Pakistan's top order simply got on with the job, whether they were sending the ball into the crowd, to the boundary rope or down to leg for a regulation single.

His Highness Sheikh Sultan bin Mohammed al Qasimi, Ruler of Sharjah and Member of the Supreme Council, entered the ground at 11.15 am. Players from both teams were presented to HH Sheikh Sultan, who then watched the game for some time. His support was unstinting in promoting cricket in the emirate.

This was a watershed match for big-time cricket in the Emirates. The cricket world watched and awaited the umpire's verdict. Sharjah passed with flying colours.

Ian Botham... where's that gone?

Graeme 'Foxy' Fowler... historic century

Countless words have been written about cricket in Sharjah since 1981, but few have summed it up better than Ian Bain, who covered this grand match between England and Pakistan. This delightful story was published in the Dubai-based Khaleej Times on Sunday, March 6, 1983. England had played Pakistan and crowds had exceeded all expectations. Offshore cricket was here to stay. This is how Bain recorded the day:

"The little Pakistani perched precariously on top of the high wall which surrounds Sharjah Cricket Stadium. He wobbled back and forth for a few moments then, urged on by the many behind him, closed his eyes, gulped and launched himself.

He plopped to the ground and lay spread-eagled for an uncomfortably long time before scrambling to his feet and running to the fence which separated him from the heroes of the Pakistan cricket team who were performing equally dangerous feats out in the middle.

It was the kind of day which prompted acts of bravado on and off the field as disappointed fans scrambled for entry and the players scrambled for runs.

The Rothmans Trophy one-day international between England and Pakistan captured the attention of the expatriate public in the way no sporting event in the Emirates ever has or possibly ever will.

Even the organisers, the Cricketers' Benefit Fund Series, were pleasantly surprised by the response. "Fantastic. That's the only word to describe it," said M.U. Haq, a member of the CBFS executive committee.

Legally and illegally, the crowd set a hard-to-beat attendance record for the relatively new Sharjah Stadium, proving that the word 'capacity' can take on a whole new and elastic meaning when a few thousand Pakistani fans show their determination. More than 12,000 crammed into the stadium which had previously been thought capable of hold-ing only 10,000. They lined the railings, the perimeter walls and roared proof of their presence six times an over.

Outside the ground, another 5,000 too old or timid to crash the party by scaling the heights, took solace in the noise from the inside and the proximity of men touched with greatness.

"You must understand the attitudes to cricketers in Pakistan," former Test captain Asif Iqbal said. "They are treated like idols."

It was not an attitude, however, shared by Graeme Fowler who showed very little respect for the Pakistani bowlers as he battered their deliveries all over the ground, 12 times to the boundary.

Not that his magnificent century did England a lot of good in the long run - other than save them from embarrassment - for amid the rockets and car horns and the forests of fluttering white and green, the hawks of Pakistan lingered only fleetingly with the prey.

Miandad and Zaheer then devoured Jesty as if he was recommended by the chef while Botham could do little with ball or bat, apart from deliver a catch to Mansoor while he was trying to disturb the tranquility of the VIP box with a six into its middle.

The mighty Imran summed up his thoughts on the game when he almost effortlessly concluded the affair by hitting the gangling Cowans into the crowd and in the process thoroughly confused the score-keepers who had believed the match to be over with the previous ball.

Then it was the crowd's turn to show their approval and a certain agility as they risked serious personal damage by hurtling the railings in an effort to get to the players who were hot-footing towards the security of the pavilion.

But it was a day in which there were no losers. England, relieved and relaxed after the disappointments and frustrations of their over-long visit to Australia and New Zealand, spent their visit to Sharjah in a fairly constant state of celebration or commiseration, depending on the mood of the moment.

Pakistan employed their usual business-like approach with a solid performance at the wicket and a diplomatic one off the field, in the manner of those who very much want to be asked back.

But back to Fowler. It was Neville Cardus who described a particular cricketer as "holding all summers in his stroke". In Sharjah on Friday, the Lancashire batsman contained a large amount of the UAE's spring as he added glory to an already spectacular occasion. And he endeared himself even more to the hugely receptive audience when he crossed the ropes, dismissed by Imran for 108, and handed his bat to a young spectator, Asim Malik. It was the kind of stuff that schoolboy's dreams are made of.

In the press box a reporter from a local Arab newspaper turned to an Englishman, admitted his inability to understand any part of the proceedings and asked for an instant explanation. What he heard didn't seem to justify his editor's insistence on his presence and he argued: "But the game of cricket doesn't have a result, does it?"

The Englishman replied that occasionally it did. It might have helped the reporter's new-found knowledge if he'd refrained from adding that, on delightful days like Friday, a result didn't really matter."

It had also been the heroes of Pakistan to the fore mid-week when Imran Khan and Javed Miandad won the double-wicket competition. Kapil Dev and Sandeep Patil finished a close second with the great Clive Lloyd and Bill Bourne flying the flag for the West Indies in third spot. Sharjah's Humayun Sumar and Mohammed Munir were fourth, with England's greatest all-rounder Ian Botham and Graham Stevenson fifth, followed by Dubai's Saleem Iqbal and Zahid Hussein. Sixes were, of course, the order of the day and the event featured some furious hitting, particularly from Kapil, Botham and Lloyd. The most dangerous job in the UAE was that of a taxi driver pulling up outside Sharjah Stadium.

Clive Lloyd hits out

CHAPTER 6

WORLD CUP RUNNETH OVER

And so to April, 1984, the Orwellian year, and the first Asia Cup, billed as the richest tournament in cricket history. It would be under the searching spotlight of the world's cricket nations and media. No cricket spectacle on this scale had been mounted in the UAE.

India held the World Cup and would be highly fancied, but their fans in the UAE held their collective breath because their heroes had been mauled by the West Indies. There would be no West Indies at this tournament, but Pakistan were flying in, as were Sri Lanka. Pakistan had struggled in Australia recently, but felt confident about this event while the Sri Lankans' fortunes fluctuated on a recent tour of New Zealand.

It was another banner season. Where else would you have found an organisation putting up $100,000 - huge prize-money in those days - to support a game which did not have a large local player and fan base? There was $50,000 for the winners, $30,000 to the runners-up and $20,000 for the last team. But still, the fact that the game was being played in the Middle East at the Sharjah stadium - more than that, was doing well - never ceased to amaze visitors to the Emirates, as well as many residents.

A new turf wicket was laid and there would be plenty of runs in it, according to Asif Iqbal, who was also quick to refute that too much money was coming into the tournaments in Sharjah. He argued that staging such an event was a huge logistical exercise. Also, the respective Boards of Control had sanctioned the Asia Cup, making it a fully-fledged tournament.

"Nothing beats the prestige of winning an international tournament. National pride is such a strong thing," said Iqbal.

In the end, it was all India. The Asia Cup went in the showcase with the World Cup. India outclassed Sri Lanka in Sharjah, although the Sri Lankans had disposed of powerful Pakistan with relative ease.

The match to decide the Cup saw India restricted to four for 188 in a 46-over match. Opening batsman Surinder Khanna scored 56, his second half-century in as many innings during which he hit two sixes off Abdul Qadir. India got bogged down, but in the last eight overs it was Sunny all over Pakistan. The two Sunnys, Gavaskar and Patil, put on 57 precious runs.

Sunil Gavaskar at his elegant best

Patil, who hit a gigantic six off Safraz Nawaz, was out for 43 on the last ball of the innings. Gavaskar carried his bat for 36.

Patil, noted for the fluency, flair and sheer power of his driving, cutting and hooking, was one of the most extraordinarily gifted players ever to ply his trade in Sharjah. The successful pop singer, actor and businessman could take apart any attack in the world, and frequently did. Few in Australia will forget his awesome 174 against Australia in the Adelaide Test of 1980/1. Len Pascoe had struck the attacking right-hander a brutal blow on the head in the previous Test. When Patil hit 129 in a Test against England in 1982, the innings included 18 fours… six of them coming from an over by Bob Willis that included a no-ball. This equalled the highest number of runs scored off one Test over of six legitimate balls.

Pakistan could only come up with 134 in 39.4 overs in reply. Admittedly, Javed Miandad and Wasim Raja failed fitness tests, but Pakistan's effort appeared decidedly half-hearted. And Pakistan's cause wasn't helped by the curious approach of opener Mohsin Khan and number three Mudassar Nazar. The pair batted as if they were trying to save a Test rather than win a one-dayer. Mohsin had already run out his opening partner Saadat Ali (13), a talented youngster with sound technique who was seeing the ball well.

Mohsin's innings of 35 took 23 overs, but that was positively quick-fire compared to Mudassar's 19-over stay for only 18 runs. Four suicidal run–outs took away the rest of Pakistan's initiative. Three wickets fell in successive balls, two to run-outs. Roger Binny and Ravi Shastri kept the ball in the slot and each was rewarded with three wickets.

Khanna was man-of-the-match and man-of-the-tournament. Scorched-earth out-cricket won this tournament for India, a team of unyielding spirit and now clearly the best ODI side in the world.

Sharjah fans cheer their heroes

CHAPTER 7

BORDER WAR

For nearly a century the Australians helped to paint the global canvas of cricket with flair, zest and competitiveness. Obviously Middle East fans wanted to see the current team, Allan Border's men, in Sharjah. Would the Aussies come to Sharjah and join India, Pakistan and England in a four-nations Rothmans Cup pre-summer 1985?

The affinity of the emirate and the CBFS with the subcontinent, of course, ran deep, hence India and Pakistan being in Sharjah quite a lot. Another England visit to Sharjah was a coup, but England was less than seven hours away by plane and the national team had competed with distinction at Sharjah Stadium a year previously. In addition, English players such as Mike Gatting, Graham Roope, Pat Pocock, Mark Nicholas, John Lever, Ian Botham and Keith Fletcher often played in the region, particularly at Sharjah, in the double-wicket competitions and with the touring Barbican sides. But the Aussies ... that really would be something.

"No, too far," said the sceptics.

The rumours persisted. Then it was confirmed, the Australians were on their way. Offshore cricket made a quantum leap. The visit by the Aussies would be genuine proof of the expanding strength of and deepening respect for the CBFS.

A few months earlier in Australia, pounded by the might of the West Indies, Kim Hughes - in despair, frustration and loneliness - decided to step down from the greatest job in the Antipodes, that of captain of his country's cricket team. Only 42 men have led Australia in Tests. One of those is Allan Border, who replaced Hughes.

Border and his men flew to the Gulf.

Australian umpire Mel Johnson was delayed quite some time at Dubai airport explaining that box of red things with stitching and peculiar bird logos. Kookaburra cricket balls were still not as well known in the Gulf as in Johnson's native Queensland.

Inside a five-star hotel where a waterfall cascaded from the first floor and birds flew around the foyer, Border, the pugnacious Australian captain who went on to became the greatest run-scorer in Test history, talked to the author about Sharjah, himself and his team.

"The Tests are still the greatest contest," he said.

"But the crowds love the one-day game and it boosts the sport so much. Sharjah is a superb thing because it takes our sport to a new area, to new people."

Border went down to the ground to have a look at the all-important square. There was not a blade of grass. The Aussies had two spinners in the touring party, but Border realised he would be rolling his arm over too. Manager Bob Merriman commented that the wicket "is obviously going to take a bit of spin." Just a bit.

Allan Border keeps one out

Although not a big turner of the ball, Border said: "Spin will be particularly important. We've got good spinners (Murray Bennett and Greg Matthews), but I can be just as hard to hit as those guys and it could be a big help on the day. I'll be doing a bit of bowling."

There was huge interest in Border's men because within six weeks an Ashes tour would be in full swing. Press interest was heightened because Hughes, in the side for Sharjah, was left out of the squad to tour England in the fight for the Ashes. However, the bulk of the squad in the UAE would take on England at home after facing England in Sharjah. So a mini-Ashes dress rehearsal with all the traditional needle, was set to unfold.

There was also the matter of two of the best Indian and Pakistani teams ever to be assembled.

The grand English journalist Frank Keating came to Sharjah to run an eye over the Australian team, as did Tony Lewis, the Welshman who had skippered England. The eloquent Michael Coward, then of the Melbourne Age and Sydney Morning Herald was in the UAE, also Steve Robilliard, of Sydney's Channel 7. Leading journalists from India and Pakistan were now regulars in Sharjah.

"We were totally fascinated with the idea of top-class cricket being played in the desert in the Gulf," Robilliard said. Coward has a long-standing love affair with the subcontinent so he was keen to see this new venue where many of his friends were playing.

Some players new to the northern hemisphere wore the baggy green cap. One was a gangling young country boy from rural Queensland with a long run and a wild action. He was fast and his name was Craig McDermott. The 19-year-old had been prepared to fight fire with fire against the West Indies.

Equally exciting was Wasim Akram, a tall, left-arm quick and big-hitting tail-ender who snared five wickets in each innings in the recent Dunedin Test against New Zealand. "I've got a long way to go before I regard myself as an international-class bowler," said Akram, who was to return to Sharjah nearly two decades later as the only bowler in the world to take 300 one-day wickets and one of the select few to take 400 in Tests.

Then there was a gawky lad from Hyderabad who, in one amazing month, carved out a slice of immortality. Mohammed Azharuddin hit 110 in his first Test, against England in Calcutta, then in the second Test, in Madras, he scored 105. 'Azhar' became only the fourth man - and first

Wasim Akram... bowling dynamo

Indian - to achieve such a feat. The third Test in Kanpur saw Azharuddin knock up 122, the only player in history to score three centuries in a row, including on debut.

Mobile phones hadn't been invented back then. Fifteen years later India's cricket authorities handed down a life ban to Azharuddin for match fixing when he admitted to helping rig three one-day internationals. Azharuddin, who was to become India's most successful captain, missed the chance to play his 100th Test match. He became the world's first cricketer to be stranded on 99 appearances.

How many times, Kapil Dev was wondering in Sharjah mid-1985, did India have to prove their position as the greatest team in international one-day cricket in the early 1980s? Victory in the Rothman's Trophy final was aimed at silencing the few remaining doubters.

"Our win in the World Cup in 1983 was, at that time, the greatest moment of my cricketing career," Kapil said during a break in net practice at the Sharjah Cricket Stadium. "Then came the (World Series) victory in Melbourne just a few weeks ago. We've won against the best in the world twice now, despite everyone thinking we couldn't do it."

Kapil, back in charge of the Indian team after two years, added: "What we've done is show that our performances were no flukes."

The opening game was an out-and-out classic. The famous former Indian all-rounder Ravi Shastri rates it is one of the greatest matches he was involved in.

The clash produced one of the most devastating spells of pace bowling Imran Khan ever unleashed on any ground in the world. On a wicket offering absolutely nothing the wonderful all-rounder tore the heart out of the Indian batting line up.

Imran nailed Shastri lbw for a first-ball duck. After that came fellow opener Srikkanth (6), then

Vengsarkar (1), Gavaskar (2) and Amarnath (5). It was an amazing first spell. Imran also picked up big-hitter Madan Lal (11) down the order. This was thoroughbred Imran, with his model action, at his absolute bowling peak. His figures read 10-2-14-6.

A typically fluent 47 by Azharuddin prevented total embarrassment for India. He was eventually deceived in the air and bowled by Tauseef Ahmed. Kapil Dev hit out, but was bowled by Tauseef.

India were all out for 125 from 42.4 overs. This would be a cakewalk for a Pakistani batting line-up boasting Mudassar Nazar, Mohsin Khan, Rameez Raja, Javed Miandad, Ashraf Ali, Imran and Saleem Malik.

Pakistan were doing it easy. Amarnath did blast the stumps to run out Mohsin on 10, but India didn't seem to be able to capitalise on the breakthrough. Mudassar was joined by Rameez Raja and the pair put on 35. Roger Binny got one to move away from Mudassar (18) and Gavaskar took the first of his four catches with a brilliant dive to his right. A few jitters for Pakistan.

Shastri, fresh from being crowned Champion of Champions in the World Series in Australia, picked up the blue-chip wicket of Javed for a duck, Gavaskar holding another great catch. Two more ducks followed: Ashraf and Imran, both victims of

Mike Gatting arrives in the Gulf

Sivaramakrishnan, the brilliant young leggie.

Pakistan had been 40 without loss. Now they were reeling at five for 50.

There was plenty of work to be done, but the big guns did it. Kapil, back on for his second spell, bagged Rameez for 29 when Gavaskar held yet another sharp chance, then Taheer Naqqash went.

There's hardly a match been played that Saleem Malik couldn't save, despite all the scandal later on. Not this one though. Sivaramakrishnan and Shastri landed the ball on the spot and gave nothing away. Malik was dismissed for 17, another to fall to Shastri's bowling and Gavaskar's immaculate hands.

Madan Lal caught-and-bowled Mansoor Elahi and Kapil capped an outstanding bowling performance by sending Tauseef Ahmed's stumps flying.

In taking two wickets Shastri bowled his full 10 overs, sent down five maidens and conceded only 17 runs. Sivaramakrishnan's figures were 7-2-16-2. Big-hearted Kapil had three for 17 off 6.5 overs.

Pakistan fell for 87, an extraordinary 38 runs short. Never had Imran bowled a more inspired spell. Shrugging off injury and coming off his full run, man-of-the-match honours were of little consolation to the marauding Imran as India marched on.

The action was then handed over to two other traditional cricket foes. Border's spin prophecy came through when Australia needed a win against England after failing against India. This game is still recalled as one of the best ever played at Sharjah Stadium. Graeme Fowler, who loved batting there, scored a neat 26 before edging to Kim Hughes off seamer Terry Alderman, but Tim Robinson, in tremendous recent Test form, edged the live-wire spinner Greg Matthews to Steve Rixon behind the stumps. Spinners Bennett, Matthews and Border took six of the wickets - unusual for one-day cricket in the 1980s - with Border's analysis reading 7-0-21-3.

On a wicket where dust flew when the ball landed, Australia kept England to eight for 177 in 50 overs.

Australia got away well enough thanks to the experienced pair of left-handers, Kepler Wessels, the South African expatriate, and West Australian Graeme Wood. The pair put on 54 for the first wicket with Wood in top form.

Spin prevailed when Phil Edmonds bowled Wessels for 16. Giant Derek Pringle had Wood caught behind by French when he was looking particularly dangerous at 35. Wood lofted two sixes (the first of the tournament) and hit two fours. Big-hitting Dean Jones (27) holed out to Moxon off Edmonds. Everyone was getting a few, including eventual man-of-the-match Matthews who scored 24.

Australia inched closer and with wickets in hand. England, particularly Richard Ellison in his second spell, bowled a tight line. However, while Simon O'Donnell, one of the hardest hitters in the one-day game (just *how hard* Sharjah was to see five years later when the Victorian blasted his way into the record books) was at the wicket Australia were well in it. Ellison picked up the vital wicket of O'Donnell for 19.

Showdown.

Australia need seven runs from six balls. Ellison, Afro-haired and with huge shoulders and capable of genuine pace, measured out his long run. 'Keeper Steve Rixon was on strike, pace bowler Rod McCurdy at the other end. Rixon stole a single. McCurdy hit a two. The third was a dot ball. McCurdy pushed Ellison for another two, then he hit a single off the fifth delivery.

Scores tied, one ball to go. Rixon, a competent batsman who scored a century in Australia's domestic Sheffield Shield competition, was on strike. He told McCurdy, "run whatever happens".

Surprisingly for Sharjah, a hush descended over the crowd, so tense was the atmosphere. Then the crowd of 8,000-plus started cheering. It reached a crescendo when Ellison delivered the ball. Rixon turned the good-length ball to mid-wicket and bolted. A shy at the stumps missed, but the man nicknamed 'Stumper' would have been home anyway. Rixon kept running, all the way to the pavilion gate.

Border said: "I thought we had lost it when O'Donnell went, but our men had the tenacity to fight on."

Yet it was a slick India who reigned supreme with a three-wicket win in the trophy final. And all-rounder Mohinder Amarnath rekindled memories of the World Cup victory over the West Indies at Lord's where he was also man-of-the-match. Amarnath was undefeated on 24 in the Sharjah final and had chipped in with the two key wickets of Border and Hughes.

Wood had a nasty habit of getting run out in big matches and it happened again, after he put together a stylish 27. The compact Wessels scored 30 before Gavaskar took his fifth catch of the series, this time from Madan Lal's bowling. Jones (8) went to Madan Lal, but Border (27) and Hughes (11) looked set for big

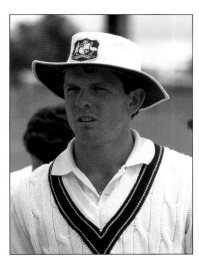

Speed man Craig McDermott

scores until Amarnath's spell. Remarkably, Hughes and Border were both caught and bowled.

The middle-order collapse, an unfortunate trademark of Australian sides throughout the 1980s, left the Aussies reeling at five for 115. Mathews dug in but no-one stayed with him and the team's cause wasn't helped by the run-outs of O'Donnell and Rixon. Australia were all out for 139 in 42.3 overs.

Border, in his first series as skipper on foreign soil, wasn't surrendering the final. India were forced to make heavy weather of the chase. McDermott worked up plenty of pace and also got his swing and cut working. A gem of an in-cutter trapped Srikkanth lbw. The Aussies could see daylight when O'Donnell had Shastri caught behind for nine.

Azharuddin played some delightful shots, including a flick to the square-leg boundary off McDermott. He tried it again next ball and Jones held the catch, shades of the first match of the tournament when McDermott picked up Azharuddin cheaply with the Victorian holding a screamer at square leg.

Azharuddin, hailed the best young batsman in the world, couldn't seem to keep that flick to leg on the ground. McDermott, after getting him the first time, said: "He looks a good

Allan Border cuts a ball down to third man

bat, but he's got a weakness there and I know I can get him again."

It may have been on Azharuddin's mind when the sides met in the final - it was certainly on McDermott's - because he was out for 22 to the big fast bowler. Azharuddin scored a lot of runs against Australia over the years but always found McDermott difficult and some feel it dated back to Sharjah when the two boom colts first squared off in Sharjah.

Gavaskar and Vengskarkar, who batted with a runner and had a life before he got off the mark, steadied the innings. But the Aussies dug deep. Gavaskar, who

Terry Alderman... accuracy personified

hit two boundaries in scoring 20, was run out and Vensarkar played on to an inspired McDermott. The Indians were five for 103.

Matthews and Murray Bennett, his spin partner from New South Wales, kept up the pressure. Kapil looked decidedly uncomfortable against the spin and it didn't surprise when Mathews clean bowled him. Mathews then bowled Binny for two.

Twenty runs were required for victory. Amarnath, who simply relished situations like this, guided India home. Madan Lal slammed the winning runs with a four off Border. McDermott, who bowled so well, was rewarded with the figures of 10-0-36-3.

It was a surprise to many when Gavaskar won the $5,000 man-of-the-series award, mainly on the strength of his catching. Mathews, the choice of most, received a 'special prize' of $1,000.

Kapil said the final was tough despite Australia being in the rebuilding stage following the retirements of Dennis Lillee, Greg Chappell and Rod Marsh. The Indian skipper revealed that his team's long hours working on fielding and fitness proved the difference in one-day tournaments around the world in recent times.

"We have worked particularly hard on athletics training and fitness exercises and the results speak for themselves. There is always the element of luck, but if a side holds its catches and stops the hits, it obviously stands a better chance of winning."

Pakistan defeated England by 43 runs in the play-off for third place. Javed walloped 71 and 41-year-old England skipper Norman Gifford bowled magnificently to take four for 23.

Border was philosophical after his first Sharjah sojourn.

"We'd have liked to have won the final, but that's one-day cricket."

Viv Richards and Kapil Dev prepare for the toss in Sharjah

CHAPTER 8

VIV-TORIOUS

Sharjah made great strides in a few short years, but one piece of the jigsaw was missing. The breeze of a rumour grew stronger, and soon Sharjah was hit by a Force 10 Caribbean hurricane. The missing piece was filled when the great West Indies came to Sharjah for the hugely successful Rothman's Challenge Cup in November 1985 .

India and Pakistan were Sharjah regulars while the auld enemy, Australia and England, were recent additions to the roster.

Yet as the dust settled on the tournament earlier in the year the Arab world's unique and enterprising cricket entrepreneur, Abdulrahman Bukhatir, told the Rothman's Trophy prize-giving dinner: "The only thing we haven't got is the West Indies ... and we hope to have them soon."

Like all else in the amazing Sharjah success story, the dream became a scheme and the scheme was soon turned into reality. Clive Lloyd had just relinquished the West Indies captaincy, but he was brought to the tournament anyway as a CBFS beneficiary.

The wonderful West Indies, captained by Viv Richards, who fears God and nothing else, swaggered into the Gulf for the first time and destroyed India by eight wickets in the decisive match of the three-nation Rothman's Challenge Cup Tournament. Again, no final was played, the championship being decided on run-rate if necessary.

India arrived in Sharjah as holders of every major one-day cricket title in the world, including the 'big three': the World Cup, World Series and the Rothman's Trophy. But since had come the ignominy of a bleak tour of Sri Lanka. And the West Indies had beaten India on the five occasions they had met in one-dayers since the frenzied World Cup Final at Lord's in 1983.

The West Indies, clear favourites for the tournament, beat Pakistan in a tight opening match that produced some magnificent cricket. Mohsin Khan compiled a workmanlike 86 not out to ensure Pakistan would be competitive. Pakistan belted 54 runs off the last five overs to certainly give Richards' team something to chase, 197. Of the 54 runs, 22 came in the last over when Imran got stuck into Joel Garner, hitting 'Big Bird' for three sixes.

West Indies overhauled the 197 thanks to a wonder-

Viv Richards smashes another four

ful 99 not out by young gun Richie Richardson. His 50 came up with a six off Abdul Qadir. Richardson's 99 came off 128 balls and included the six and 11 fours. Richards whipped up a half-century with five fours and the regulation six.

Kapil Dev's team wanted a confidence-boosting win over Pakistan in the side's opening match of the tournament, but that didn't happen. Only a back-to-the-wall knock of 63 by that most reliable of opening batsmen, Sunil Gavaskar, retrieved the match from total humiliation and left it merely at a 48-run loss.

The classy Pakistani side, under new skipper Imran, thwarted India's bid for a hat-trick of wins against them in Sharjah. Highlight of the Pakistan innings was a knock of 67 by Mudassar. Rameez Raja scored 66.

That victory resulted in the most extraordinary scenes witnessed in Sharjah Cricket Stadium's short history. Barricades and barriers were sent tumbling as fans ran, sang and danced. Noise from horns and drums was deafening. Fans who hoisted their heroes on their shoulders surrounded the team. Crowds sang and chanted outside their hotel for hours.

Kapil had said at the previous tournament that he had a "single-minded ambition" to have "this Indian side remembered as the greatest one-day team in the history of the game."

Leading up to the vital last match India's manager, Venkataraghavan, said: "We have beaten them earlier and we are capable of beating them again. It will, however, be a very close battle. More is expected of our batsmen this time. You must have wickets in hand for the slog later on."

The taciturn Kapil wouldn't be drawn. "I like only to play," he said.

Richards wasn't saying a lot either: "Our team is feeling fine … and confident."

Wes Hall, the West Indies manager, added: "We don't make a lot of plans - we just go out and play cricket."

West Indies made one change for the second game. Courtney Walsh, a young man destined for greatness, replaced Anthony Gray.

West Indies turned the screws straight away. Man-of-the-match Joel Garner didn't concede a run until his fifth over. His bowling analysis was 9-4-11-2. Of the 11 runs 'Big Bird' conceded, four were no-balls. New ball partner Malcolm Marshall was equally miserly, also conceding only 11 runs with four of those no-balls.

Richards hit the third ball of the 42nd over, from Rajinder Singh Ghai's bowling, for a six over mid-wicket to win the match.

The three-way tie would have been decided on run-rate if India won, but that was never a possibility. India's batting was too slow, just too slow. Supporters were stunned that Kapil's men could post only four for 180. Gavaskar scored an unbeaten 76, but much of the blame for the defeat was put down to his slow batting. He scored his second run of the innings after 40 minutes, having faced 23 deliveries.

Much had been expected of big-hitting Krishna Srikkanth, but he was out in Garner's second over. India might have done better had Kapil batted up the order as the great all-rounder ran out of partners and was not out on 28.

The West Indies batsmen had few problems knocking over the small total. Richardson made 72 to scoop all player-of-the-tournament and man-of-the-series awards. Plucky Desmond Haynes, who battled a bad cold and batted in two sweaters in the Sharjah heat, rattled up 72 and was up the other end when Richards (not out 24) smashed the six to end proceedings. This was a West Indies victory at its intimidating, professional best.

Richards said after the last game: "India are the official one-day champions. They beat us then, so it's nice to for us to beat them now. I always believe the sweetest victory is the one achieved on foreign soil. India and Pakistan have played here before and are used to the conditions, but this was our first chance to play in Sharjah. I feel very happy emerging victorious in an atmosphere completely alien to us."

Richie Richardson had emerged as the next West Indies batting genius. His skipper and fellow Antiguan, said: "Richie is one of the coolest guys I've seen. He's got four Test centuries to his credit already and he'll get even better with the passage of time. I would have loved to have played some of the shots he played today."

A disappointed Kapil Dev would only say: "It's all in the game."

CHAPTER 9

JAVED: NEVER SAY DIE

Javed Miandad belted Chetan Sharma into the wide blue yonder on the last ball of the day to give Pakistan a one-wicket win over India in the final of the five-nation Australasia Cup, the biggest and most ambitious tournament ever staged at Sharjah.

Four runs were needed for a win, with Miandad on strike. This is the man of whom Greg Chappell once remarked, "If you want someone to bat for your life, Javed Miandad is the man to do it."

It was one of those miracle moments, savoured long after stumps are drawn. Who else got runs or wickets hardly seems relevant. Everyone remembers this match in April 1986 as "the game Javed won when he hit Chetan Sharma into the crowd off the last ball."

Javed scored a remarkable century as the pride of Pakistan fell around him. Pakistan, who had never won a final in Sharjah, needed 11 runs off the last over to win this one.

Imran won the toss and invited Kapil's men to bat. The decision seemed to backfire as Srikkanth and Gavaskar, two champions, raced to 50 in only 11.4 overs. In 32.3 overs they posted 100. It got worse for Pakistan when wicketkeeper Zulqarnain dropped the dangerous Srikkanth on 51 when he failed to read Qadir's wrong 'un. Qadir got his revenge, but not until Srikkanth was 75. The classy opener had hit eight fours and towering sixes.

Gavaskar and Vengskarkar did well, the former nudging a century and the latter posting 50. But for some reason India seemed to panic. Then they definitely panicked. Eight wickets tumbled.

In reply to a total of 245, Imran's charges couldn't develop partnerships. Miandad, however, was in great touch and, as ever, wasn't going down without a fight.

Fans yelled all day. In the last over there was deathly silence punctuated by screaming applause, depending on where allegiances lay.

Sharma bowled the first ball of the last over. Miandad stroked it away and completed two runs, but Wasim Akram didn't. Miandad was still on strike. He belted the second ball for four and picked up a single off the third. Sharma sent Zulqarnain's stumps flying with his fourth ball.

Miandad was desperate for the strike. Tauseef managed to chip the fifth ball over the close-in fielders. A

Javed Miandad... historic six

27

record crowd of 20,000 watched Miandad open his shoulders and crack the last ball, a full toss, high over the mid-wicket boundary. Security and organisers couldn't hold back the fans.

The five-nation Australasia Cup was a huge venture for the CBFS and carried prize money of $110,000, but the organisation and innovation could not be faulted. Seating at the stadium, financed entirely from Bukhatir's own pocket, was expanded to 20,000.

For the first time allotted overs were 50, not 45. The team losing by the biggest margin in the quarter finals was eliminated. Sri Lanka were given a bye on the strength of the win several days before in Colombo in the Asia Cup final. The side losing by the biggest margin thereby cleared the way for the Sri Lankan side's slot.

India were first pitted against New Zealand. The Kiwis were missing a number of stars, including Richard Hadlee, Jeremy Coney, John Wright, Bruce Edgar and Ian Smith. But Martin Crowe, rated as one of the top three batsmen in the world, was in the side.

Kapil Dev had said: "We're mentally prepared to win the Cup. We are ready to face any challenge."

At the start of the tournament Pakistan had to face a new-look Australia skippered by veteran spinner Ray Bright. Allan Border withdrew from the Sharjah tour due to family commitments.

India beat the Kiwis, but any thoughts of Jeff Crowe's team being easy-beats went right out the window in a 50-over match reduced to 44 overs for each team after it was interrupted for rain, of all things.

New Zealand scored a paltry eight for 132 in 44 overs. India made heavy weather of reaching the target, being seven for 134 in 41.4 overs. Quality line-and-length bowling by Ewen Chatfield secured him three wickets for 14 runs and man-of-the-match honours.

Pakistan recorded one of their biggest one-day victories with an eight-wicket hammering of Australia. The scale of the Aussies' capitulation put them out of the tournament. Greg Ritchie (60 not out) was the pick of the Australian batsmen as the team finished with seven for 202 in 50 overs. Pakistan reeled in the total for the loss of only two wickets thanks to Mudassar Nazar (95), Mohsin Khan (46) and Rameez Raja (56 not out).

Sri Lanka gave India a wake-up call before the World Champions went through to the final. India reached a nine for 205 target with five balls to spare after a major middle order collapse.

Pakistan bundled out New Zealand for 64 runs in 35.5 overs, the Kiwis' lowest one-day total in their history. The side from the 'Shaky Isles' was shaky in batting technique as well and had no answer to either Wasim Akram's swing or Abdul Qadir's spin. So tight was the bowling that Ken Rutherford was at the crease for 40 minutes and faced 31 balls yet only managed two runs. Qadir spun a web of four wickets for only nine runs in 10 overs with four maidens.

"This was Qadir at his brilliant best," said Imran.

India knocked up 245 runs in the final, a healthy total, although by no means out of reach. Imran and Akram had bowled outstanding second spells which prevented too much big-hitting in the so-called 'slog' overs.

As cricket lovers reflect on two decades of sensational sport at Sharjah, few can cite a better match than 'Javed's final.' "It's certainly one of the best games I've played in, anywhere in the world," says Ravi Shastri. "I'll never forget the excitement out there. But it was a special era back then. That match sums up the spirit of so many thrilling contests in the 1980s."

CHAPTER 10

WALSH – THE WINDIES' WHIRLWIND

Issac Vivian Alexander Richards scored runs with the remorseless and relentless efficiency of a machine. So did his team, and they were committed to domination of world cricket.

Desmond 'The Hammer' Haynes … easy-going, chatty. Gordon Greenidge …brooding, taciturn. Both hard-hitting and of impeccable technique. The finest pair of opening batsmen on the planet.

Malcolm Marshall … totally dedicated to the cause, terrifying even on the deadest of wickets. Marshall could make a ball swing through the surf or bounce on the sands of the Empty Quarter in Saudi Arabia. (This delightful man was to become a cancer victim at the tragically young age of 38.)

Courtney Walsh … a rangy youngster never averse to doing the hard work by bowling into the wind. He became the game's greatest wicket taker. Opening batsmen took guard knowing they would face Caribbean cricket's version of a broadside from a battleship.

To sit in the stands at Sharjah for the Champions Trophy of December 1986 was to witness one of the most special periods for the West Indies. The era was started by 'Supercat' Clive Lloyd and carried on by Richards, or 'Smokin Joe.'

India, Pakistan and Sri Lanka were swept aside by the West Indies as the Caribbean machine took maximum points in another tournament that did not see the two top teams progress to a final.

West Indies thrashed Pakistan by nine wickets. The Indian team put up a fight, but was well beaten.

The pitch for the West Indies-Pakistan encounter was so dead it made the proverbial dodo seem positively flighty. Sir Donald Bradman used to say: "When you win the toss and it's a good wicket you bat. If it's a bad wicket, think about it for a few minutes … and then bat."

Mudassar Nazar and Salim Yousuf walked through the gate and out to a pitch that should have been a gold mine.

But the West Indies bowlers were of such calibre and character that a dead wicket only meant the task would be more difficult, but the result the same. Marshall, Walsh, Anthony Gray and Winston Benjamin didn't allow the Pakistani batsmen any

Courtney Walsh, the leading Test wicket-taker in history

Gordon Greenidge, the legendary opening batsman

breathing space. Yousuf was out for one, Gus Logie taking a tremendous catch from Gray's bowling. Was there a better close-in fielder than Logie at his peak? He took three catches in this match and ran out two batsmen, one of them being Javed Miandad, who rarely got it wrong between wickets.

Pakistan were painfully slow, crawling to 31 in 16 overs. Mudassar was 73 minutes at the crease, scoring 14 runs from 58 balls. Logie grabbed another catch, this time from Benjamin's bowling, to put Mudassar – and the crowd – out of some of their misery.

Rameez Raja plodded his way to 44 in 138 minutes before being caught and bowled by Walsh. The big paceman's flying, one-handed reflex catch is still one of the best taken at Sharjah.

Pakistan were never beaten while Javed was at the wicket and there was plenty of determination as he went to the crease carrying his country's colours, and hopes. Javed got to 32 and looked his usual composed self. Rameez turned a ball to square leg and opted to take a chance on Logie's arm. *Zing.* Jeff Dujon had the bails off with Javed well short.

Walsh was the pick of a great bowling attack with figures that read 9.4-1-31-4.

Greenidge (74) and Haynes (59 not out), professional men, went out and finished off the opposition. But Wasim Akram, with some determined, controlled swing, served notice he would be a thorn in the West Indies side for many years. Akram conceded only 26 runs from nine overs and should have had Greenidge's wicket, but Tauseef Ahmed dropped the champion opener on 15. Everyone was back in the pavilion in 33.2 overs. Logie was man-of-the-match.

If the Pakistan versus West Indies match was humiliation, the game against Sri Lanka was a massacre. The steel drums rolled. The records tumbled.

Richards said he wanted to leave town with a "100 per cent record."

Haynes pulled out of the match, but Richie Richardson opened with Greenidge and stroked his way to the first century of the tournament. He was put down twice early on, but the 120-ball knock, including eight fours and a six, showed why he was being hailed as the 'new Viv.' Greenidge hit 69, Richards 39. Total: 248 in 45 overs.

No-one was prepared for the onslaught that followed. The Sri Lankans were all out for 55 in only 28.3 overs. The West Indies of the mid-1980s had a habit of sending opposing teams home for convalescence.

Walsh took five wickets, four clean bowled, to walk off the field with the astonishing ODI figures of 4.3-3-1-5.

The quick bowler's spell sent Sri Lanka into the ignominy of 'worst ever' annals which statisticians are so fond of waving around when players are trying to slip quietly from the ground. Walsh's haul was the second best at Sharjah behind Imran's six for 14 a touch over a year earlier.

This was Sri Lanka's lowest score at Sharjah and their lowest in ODI cricket. Rubbing further salt into their wounds was the fact it was also the second-lowest total in ODI history - that was 45 runs in 40.3 overs by Canada against England at Manchester in 1979.

Sri Lankan skipper Duleep Mendis was disappointed, but made a good point – that his side went down swinging in a bid to win the game.

"The asking rate was so great – you have to hit out in such conditions. The batsmen didn't get out to rash strokes, but they were trying to chase such a big total. There is no point staying at the wicket unless you're scoring, especially when you're facing a huge total of 248."

Richards said it wasn't straightforward pace that tore sides apart in Sharjah and elsewhere. "People believe that the West Indies are a pace machine, but it's the nagging accuracy and subtle variation that have made our bowling so effective."

The Antiguan legend refused to dance on the grave of the Sri Lankans. "They're a good side and they're improving all the time. The day isn't too far away when they're going to spring some big surprises."

And Walsh?

"This young man is improving in leaps and bounds. Soon he will worry batsmen all over the world."

Right on both counts.

Meanwhile, Pakistan's triumph over India in the last match of the Champions Trophy completed a hat-trick of wins at Sharjah Stadium under the captaincy of Imran Khan. The result of the game was purely academic because the West Indies had already put the tournament outcome beyond doubt, but there was a great deal of pride at stake.

It was another Sharjah thriller. Nothing could top the amazing scenes on the same ground earlier in the year when Javed Miandad hit a six to win the final, but this came close.

Pakistan were on top initially having bundled India out for a paltry 144. Pakistan's opening pair, Rameez Raja and Shoaib Mohammed, cruised to 50 so victory looked a formality. But India were not to be counted out just yet. An astonishing period of play saw Pakistan crash to 65 for the loss of six wickets. India's fans were cock-a-hoop. At one stage Pakistan lost four wickets for only two runs in seven deliveries. Maninder and Shastri, the spinning duo, literally turned the match in India's favour, ripping out six wickets for only 15 runs. Maninder was on a hat trick, but Imran denied it.

All-rounder Manzoor Elahi came in when Pakistan were all but gone and threw the bat at everything in an unconquered 50, arguably the best innings of his career.

Everything seemed to be going Imran's way from the moment he won the toss and sent Kapil's men in under extremely overcast conditions. The master of reverse swing, ably supported by young Akram, put India on the back foot just about from the time he measured out his run. Imran skittled Srikkanth, Gavaskar and Raman Lamba in only 11.3 overs and with just 16 runs on the board.

Rain gave India the chance to regroup on several occasions and Azharuddin (49) and Kapil (36) kept their heads down and helped India to 144. India's batsmen had taken 22.4 overs and 108 minutes to post the first 50. Kapil and Azharuddin put on another 50 in only eight overs and 30 minutes.

A fine contest, for sure, but it didn't alter the fact that the trophy was on its way to the Caribbean.

CHAPTER 11

BROAD BAT OF BRITISH BULLDOG

There is grimness and determination about the English game. So many of England's memorable triumphs have been achieved against a background of resilience and so it proved in Sharjah in the four-nation Sharjah Cup of April 1987.

Mike Gatting's England had just won the Ashes plus the two one-day competitions in Australia. But they were underdogs in Sharjah, arriving without Gatting, David Gower, Ian Botham and Allan Lamb.

Pakistan were favourites with India and Australia level-pegging for second. England, captained by spinner and strategist John Embury, would make up the numbers, according to many of the so-called experts. Pakistan had beaten the West Indies in Australia and walloped India 5-1 in a recent one-day international series in India. Granted, England did have Chris Broad in wonderful form. Broad had just been designated International Cricketer of the Year and the stubborn left-hander would open the innings with Graeme Gooch. But pundits still felt England would find the going tough in this desert campaign.

A fascinating series transpired in which India, Pakistan and England finished on equal points after Australia were bundled out early and Embury's underdogs were awarded the Cup on run-rate.

There was no hint of the excitement to come when India, spearheaded by an in-form Kapil Dev, beat England by three wickets in the first match. Kapil hit up 64 in only 54 deliveries as India reached seven for 214, overhauling England's seven for 211.

England could actually have won this match if not for poor fielding. Kapil was dropped once, as was Azharuddin (not out 24) while Srikkanth (56) had a ridiculous four lives. The total could have been even higher because Gavaskar didn't bat due to a bad back. England looked confident at the crease though, particularly Broad, a master of percentage batting who was his typically patient in compiling 60.

In matches against Pakistan and India a hapless Australia made only 176 on both occasions and were beaten both times, leaving Allan Border's men out of the title race. India turned on a run spree with Gavaskar and Azharuddin notching a record 165-run partnership. This was the best stand ever in Sharjah, eclipsing the 132 by West Indies' Gordon Greenidge and Richie Richardson against Sri Lanka in 1986. The

Chris Broad carried on his fine Ashes form when he came to Sharjah

Indians overhauled the Aussies in 42 overs, Azharuddin finishing with 84 and Gavaskar unbeaten on 78 in his 100th appearance for India in a one-day international.

Stocky David Boon, a wonderful workhorse for Australia, was the best of the losing side with 62, his second half-century in a row. Boon faced 113 balls and hit three boundaries. He batted well, but couldn't accelerate the run-rate.

Who knows what might have been had Geoff Marsh not dropped an easy catch from Gavaskar when the little opener was on eight. Ironically, Marsh took one of the best catches ever seen in Sharjah to dismiss Azharuddin.

Pakistan had great talent on tap and the team seemed impregnable in this tournament. Someone forgot to tell England. Embury's men stormed back into the Cup equation with a five-wicket victory over Pakistan. The England side rose to the occasion by bowling a tight line, batting well and piling on the pressure with slick fielding. Three of the top Pakistani batsmen were run out.

There seemed to be something in the air. Mudassar Nazar, man of the match against Australia for his exploits with bat and ball, went for only three, beautifully caught by Jack Richards off the bowling of reliable one-day campaigner Philip DeFreitas. The gate opened. Ejaz Ahmed was run out for one when a moment's hesitation was enough to stop him beating James Whitaker's sharp throw to Richards. Rameez Raja was run out on 44.

Rescue acts were nothing new to Miandad and Imran. Miandad completed the 26th half-century of his one-day career. There have been few faster runners between wickets than Miandad, but on 60 he wasn't as quick as the direct throw from Neil Fairbrother. Imran was in commanding form, making 46 runs in 65 deliveries. Richards took a gem of a catch from Foster's bowling to send the champion all-rounder back to the pavilion. The remaining batsmen contributed little to the scoreboard.

Imran and Akram unleashed a fast, sustained and accurate attack against England. Gooch, one of England's leading opening batsmen of all time, was out for three, caught by Malik off Imran. Only 18 runs came from the first 10 overs. Imran's first five-over spell conceded a mere five runs. Akram's five overs cost just 13.

But Broad looked sound while the usually fluent Tim Robinson, although short of a gallop, hung in. Qadir's introduction into the attack was the moment the batsmen chose to open up and they hit the spinning maestro for 32 runs in five overs. Next it was the turn of Manzoor Elahi and Tauseef Ahmed to be caned - Manzoor for 31 in five overs and Tauseef for 20 in only three overs.

Mudassar picked up the important wicket of Broad, who had faced 87 deliveries and hit four boundaries, caught in the deep by Ejaz for 65. But Broad had been given two lives and the damage had been done. Robinson's touch got better, but when he was on 83, in the 37th over, Qadir came back into the attack and claimed his wicket. Revenge for the earlier onslaught.

David Boon... the Australian rock

33

Whitaker swung the bat and was dropped by Qadir off Imran in what proved an extremely costly miss as he hit a forceful 44 not out. And swashbuckling Whitaker brought up the win in the finest style, with a six off Akram.

England manager Micky Stewart was elated because he now had the championship victory in his sights. "This victory should serve as a good platform for the match against Australia," Stewart said. "Considering we lost an early wicket, Robinson and Broad did a great job in putting us on the road to victory. We fielded well and took all our catches and, more importantly, we achieved those run-outs at crucial stages and that restricted Pakistan to 217. We hope to score about 240 runs against Australia tomorrow to stay in contention for the Cup."

Skipper Imran clearly wasn't as ebullient. "Our fielding was scrappy and we dropped far too many catches. Maybe the boys are tired from the tour of India. We lost the toss and in the morning the ball was swinging. If we had batted second the story could have been different. The ball was coming on to the bat easier in the afternoon. But full credit to England, they took all the catches offered and achieved three run-outs and the one that got Javed was a beauty."

England were back in business and Australia were out of contention, but the other sides could definitely win. What would have been an inconsequential clash between England and Australia assumed vital proportions. And England versus Pakistan . . . well . . .

England beat Australia by 11 runs in a magnificent game of cricket that saw Gooch lead the way with 86, well supported by that man Broad again (44) and Fairbrother (18). Gooch, who made the Australians pay for a dropped catch at 31 by Boon, faced 119 balls and hit seven fours and a six in his 180-minute stay at the crease.

England, put in by Border, scored 230 for the loss of six wickets from the allotted 50 overs, the highest total of the tournament. The Australians needed to bat well to reach such a big target so losing their first two wickets for only seven runs (Geoff Marsh 0 and Dirk Wellham 2) made the job even tougher.

Two of the greats of the Australian game, Border and Boon, decided enough was enough. Some dignity had to be salvaged from the Sharjah tour. Suddenly England's Cup aspirations were in jeopardy as the 'old firm' blazed its way to a second-wicket stand of 159. The total moved to 166 and an Australian victory

was on the cards. However, Embury brought himself into the attack and in one phenomenal over removed Boon (73) and Border (84), triggering an Australian collapse which included three run-outs. Australia couldn't quite make it, finishing nine for 219. Gooch was man-of-the-match but Embury's 10-1-38-2 didn't tell half the story.

Stewart said: "The Australians were under pressure when we gave them a good target. Allan Border and David Boon played brilliant knocks, but the run-rate was increasing from five to six to seven as the match wore on. Then we held all our catches."

Embury felt Australia would have won if Border had stayed at the crease.

"When Border and Boon were in the middle it was a matter of us plugging away. Getting those two wickets in one over was a bonus. We knew then that Australia were gone."

Australian boss Bobby Simpson was realistic. "We blew it."

The last match wasn't so close. Imran rocked India from the start, dismissing Gavaskar (0) and Azharuddin (1). Then Srikkanth (5) was gone, victim of Akram. Vengsarkar played a lone hand, defying everything this great bowling attack could hurl at him. He certainly deserved a ton, but was stranded on 95 when India were all out for 183 for the loss of eight wickets. Manoj Prabhakar (33) gave solid support to Vensarkar but a sharp run-out by substitute Shoaib Mohammed ended his aspirations.

Imran and Akram exploited the overcast conditions to the hilt. India's bowling looked tame in comparison and Pakistan reached the total in a canter, mainly thanks to half centuries by Rameez Raja and the unbeaten Miandad. Pakistan reached the target in over 42, meaning they beat India for second place and the prize-money of $25,000. Pakistan needed to win in less than 44 overs to finish above India, but be higher on the ladder than England, Imran's men had to account for Embury's outfit in 33 overs. Pakistan were not inclined to take such a risk.

Man-of-the-series was David Boon.

During the tournament rumours spread that Imran Khan would enter politics after retiring from cricket. The champion all-rounder denied it.

"They (the media) sometimes say I'm joining the film world and now they say I'm entering politics. I don't know what I am keen on joining. I have not decided."

CHAPTER 12

SUPER SHASTRI HAS WRIGHT STUFF

When the run-ups were marked out in the 1988 mid-year tournament in Sharjah no cricketer was held in higher regard anywhere the world than Richard Hadlee, later Sir Richard, the fast-bowling all-rounder with the ultimate control of pace, swing and cut.

The urbane 37-year-old equalled Ian Botham's record of 373 wickets against Australia in Melbourne in the Australian summer. He was unable to break the record because tailender Mike Whitney blocked the last six balls to force a draw in arguably the greatest trans-Tasman Test of all time. Hadlee went on to become the first man to break through the 400-wicket barrier in Tests.

Kiwi fans hoped Hadlee could inspire the national side to great things in Sharjah. New Zealand's only previous visit, without Hadlee, was for the Australasia Cup of 1986 when the Kiwis were routed for 64 in a 10-wicket semi-final hiding at the hands of a fired-up Pakistan.

Ravi Shastri performed many great feats in Sharjah

The Sharjah Cup of 1988 featured New Zealand, India and Sri Lanka.

India could muster a mere 219 in their opening game against Sri Lanka and only a sensational batting collapse by Sri Lanka saved Indian skipper Ravi Shastri's team from an embarrassing defeat. However, an inspired India marched into the final by beating New Zealand by 73 runs. Mohinder Amarnath was unconquered on 102, a superb knock that helped India to six for 267. Man-of-the-match Mohinder became the third century maker at Sharjah after Javed Miandad and Richie Richardson. Mohinder and Sidhu put on 158 runs, just one short of the record third-wicket stand put on by Australians David Boon and Allan Border against England in the previous Sharjah tournament.

New Zealand played Sri Lanka twice, in the league game then the semi-final, and won easily on both occasions. Robert Vance batted brilliantly for 96 before being run out in the 43-run semi-final win while Andrew Jones (85) and Ken Rutherford (65) were the major contributors to the 99-run victory in the league match. (Sri Lanka's Ashoka de Silva made the best of his 'home ground' advantage, taking three wickets for 38 runs from eight overs. Several years ago de Silva played in Dubai with the Lanka Lions and at Sharjah Stadium in the local Bukhatir League)

New Zealand had their moments in the final, but Shastri's men were too good and ran out winners by 52 runs. Accurate bowling kept New Zealand in with

Kapil Dev ... explosive innings

Sir Richard Hadlee, perhaps the best bowler of all time

a bit of a shout, but the Kiwis let India off the hook.

India's middle order got stuck into the bewildered Kiwis. India hit 107 runs from the last 10 overs - Kapil Dev cracked 49 not out off a mere 26 balls - to take the team to seven for 250 in the 50 overs. Even by Kapil's standards, he laid the wood on. The all-rounder topped off his knock with two leg-side sixes off Ewen Chatfield.

Chatfield, known for his nagging accuracy, saw his final two overs cost 30 runs. The great man Hadlee conceded only eight runs in his first five-over spell, but he was hit for 41 in his second five-over stint.

India had been four for 82 after 27 overs and four for 143 off 40 overs, all thanks to tight bowling and marvellous fielding. Only veteran Amarnath was seeing the ball and he put together an attractive 58.

Shastri grabbed the innings by the scruff of the neck, playing what he later described as "one of my best one-day knocks." Reaching 200 looked an uphill battle for India until Shastri exploded. He struck three sixes and three fours in his memorable 72 from 68 balls which saw him become the third Indian to score 2,000 runs in one-day cricket. Shastri and Kapil added 73 for the sixth wicket.

New Zealand skipper John Wright showed ample evidence of his quality before being run out for 55. New Zealand needed only 56 runs in the last 10 overs to win, but the tail was too long and didn't wag. Hirwani, the Indian spinner, bowled magnificently throughout the tournament and his figures for all matches were 30-1-129-10. Four of those wickets came in the final, including the dangerous Mark Greatbatch for 47.

Wright was typically gracious in defeat.

"My run out was the turning point when we were chasing the target. Earlier Shastri and Kapil cut loose to put their team on top. Those 10 overs cost us the game. I don't think our bowlers bowled well enough in the slog overs. And we didn't play Hirwani intelligently."

Man-of-the-series Hirwani's 10 wickets were more than any bowler from any side. He took four wickets in a match on two occasions, tremendous bowling in ODI cricket.

Shastri, man-of-the-match in the big game, said: "New Zealand had us on the rack before the last 10 overs, but after the 250 runs were on the board I knew we'd take it out."

CHAPTER 13

CURT RESPONSE BRINGS GREAT WINDIES WIN

In the late '80s the West Indies were the most feared and formidable Test and ODI side on earth. Seasoned professionals and minnows shared the same fate at their hands - defeat and humiliation.

The class and ferocity of the West Indies was never more in evidence than in the week-long, three-nation Sharjah Champions Trophy of October 1988.

The 'team of the '80s' retained the Sharjah Champions Trophy by beating Pakistan by 11 runs in a thrilling finish to a compelling competition.

The Calypso Kings thus completed a hat-trick of titles, but not before the globe's most feared cricket entity staged a dramatic form reversal by losing the preliminary games to India and Pakistan. Pakistan beat India and the West Indies to make the final. India triumphed over the West Indies in the opening match, but were beaten in the semi-final.

The West Indies arrived without Malcolm Marshall, the world's finest fast bowler. Marshall was particularly dangerous on wickets that did not offer much incentive to pace bowlers, such as the traditionally bare Sharjah strip. Lightning-fast Ian Bishop was the more than able replacement. Pakistan, however, were without Imran Khan.

As skipper Viv Richards said: "Marshall's loss is a big blow. He is a great player. His replacement, Ian Bishop, is a good bowler, but Malcolm is such a hard act to follow. However, we have done without Malcolm before."

Richards was disappointed that Imran decided to skip the tournament. "Imran is a great cricketer. He has been an inspiration to the Pakistan team. Players like Imran bring out the best in everyone."

Richards again claimed his team didn't simply rely on four quicks unleashing terrifying spells of fast bowling to secure results.

"Of course we have a great bunch of fast bowlers, but over the years our batting has played an equally important role in our triumphs."

He added ominously: "But if we make 80 we expect our bowlers to bowl out the opposition for less than that."

Pumped-up India and Pakistan set about bringing the West Indies down to earth.

It started with India overhauling the West Indies'

total of 239 in the first preliminary game, thanks primarily to a blazing century by the 'Tamil Nadu Typhoon', Srikkanth. India had crawled to 14 runs in the first 10 overs before Srikkanth throttled the bowling. The West Indies batsmen had struggled against the spin of Hirwani. A sprained ankle kept Richards out of the game.

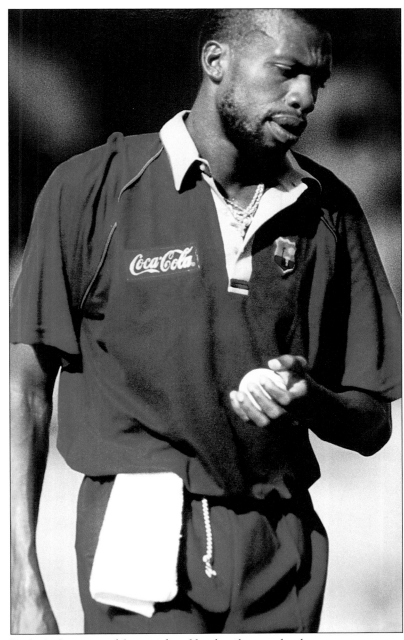

Curtly Ambrose, one of the most feared bowlers the game has known

Desmond Haynes, the Windies' power-hitter

Kapil Dev became the highest wicket-taker in one-day cricket when he claimed the wicket of Desmond Haynes. The Indian all-rounder had been level with West Indies paceman Joel Garner, both having 146 wickets to their credit before this match. Kapil equalled Garner's record at the same ground in the previous Sharjah tournament.

Pakistan cleaned up the West Indies, scoring a mammoth six for 294 then restricting them to five for 210. Every one of Pakistan's top order scored well and the feared Patrick Patterson was taken for 72 runs in eight overs. Wasim Akram turned promise into gold. In 15 deliveries he claimed Haynes (1), Richardson (6) and Hooper (0). Greenidge, a batting machine, continued to defy the attack and was unconquered on 102 at the end of play. Richards remained sidelined with injury.

The West Indies scrambled through to the final with a win over India. Greenidge would again lead the side in the decider in 'King Viv's' absence.

Miandad asked the West Indies to bat in the final.

Haynes and Greenidge raced to the fastest half-century stand of the tournament, in 60 balls. Manzoor Elahi held a wonderful catch at long leg from Mudassar's bowling to dismiss Greenidge, who batted for 75 minutes, faced 48 balls and made 37 runs. Haynes was at the crease for 138 minutes, played 90 balls and scored 45 before Malik at square leg somehow held a powerfully struck low shot off Shoaib.

The leg-spin wizardry of Abdul Qadir, brought on after only 10 over, got Richardson for two, bowled around his legs. It was a quicker ball that turned Richardson inside out and took middle and leg.

Pakistan were well in the match but the forthright and fluent Carl Hooper's 62 provided the required anchor to the innings. Hooper, aged 20 (with Test and ODI centuries to his credit) and Keith Arthurton, included for Gus Logie, added 67 valuable runs for the fourth wicket. Hooper's 62 came up in only 70 balls. 'Keeper Jeff Dujon and all-rounder Roger Harper also helped out, Dujon hitting 21 off 25 balls while Harper scored 16 from 17 deliveries.

The required run rate was 4.75, by no means out of the question, but Ambrose put Pakistan to the sword. Pakistan had no answer to Ambrose whose brilliance brought him figures of 10-0-29-4, and that was after having several catches dropped!

The rampaging fast bowler had openers Mudassar and Rameez Raja out with only 20 runs on the board. Javed joined Shoaib at the crease but Shoaib went for 15, caught Bishop bowled Walsh. Wily campaigners

Saleem Malik and Miandad, got their heads down. Big innings were needed from the duo and they kept the scoreboard ticking over with ones and twos. Malik (38) and Ijaz Ahmed (17) were dismissed, but Javed stayed put. At the 43-over mark, the two sides were neck-and-neck on 118.

Ambrose struck the killer blow in the 44th over when he bowled Miandad. The inspirational Miandad was at the crease for 116 minutes and scored 76 runs off as many balls.

Saleem Yousuf was run out next ball. Then Ambrose bowled Akram. Three wickets had gone for 10 runs. Manzoor was bowled by Patterson leaving 18 runs to

be scored off the last over with Qadir on strike. He got seven of them. Not enough.

Manager Clive Lloyd was delighted the West Indies could win without Richards and Marshall, particularly as the team was about to fly out on a searching three-month tour of Australia.

"With a tour like Australia coming up it

The heat became to much for umpire Harold 'Dickie' Bird and he had to be helped from the field

helps a great deal to be on a high, especially for the newcomers to the side. It will be a hard tour. We held Richards back because we need him to be 100 per cent fit for the campaign Down Under."

And what of Ambrose, who relished the chance to spearhead the attack? He was clearly about to step up to the big time, according to Lloyd.

"Ambrose is improving with every tour and has all the qualities of a great fast bowler. But the West Indies have had a great tradition in that respect for some time now. Every youngster wants to be a fast bowler."

English Test umpire Harold 'Dickie' Bird, 55, found the heat too much and collapsed during the final. In the Pakistani innings, Bird staggered and fell to the ground. He was stretchered from the field and attended by a doctor at the ground before being taken to hospital and treated for dehydration.

Organisers sent local association umpire Farid Malik on to the field to officiate with England's David Shepherd. For Malik, a Pakistani expatriate, it was the proverbial dream come true. He had umpired several first class matches in Pakistan, but never an international contest. The newcomer was called upon to give an interesting decision: a no-ball after spotting extra fielders on the leg side. He also adjudged Saleem Yousuf run out.

Keith Arthurton, part of the West Indies' winning formula

CHAPTER 14

MALIK-IOUS!

Saleem Malik blazed his way to one of the most fluent centuries seen in Sharjah to help inflict a seven-wicket defeat on Sri Lanka in the Asia Cup decider of March 1989. There were only the two teams in this tournament and Pakistan had little difficulty beating Sri Lanka in either match.

Saleem Malik... Sharjah run-feast

Pakistan, also the holders of the Australasia Cup, defeated Sri Lanka by 30 runs in the opening encounter. Sri Lanka gave their all in the second match, scoring 244 for the loss of eight wickets. They also bowled and fielded with plenty of enthusiasm.

Sri Lanka's skipper Arjuna Ranatunga won the toss and elected to bat in the crucial second encounter. Intentions were clear when Roshan Mahanama sent Imran's first ball of the day to the boundary. The opening pair of Mahanama and Kuruppu maintained the brisk pace.

Pakistan looked likely to pay dearly for dropping Kuruppu on 10. Imran and Aquib, two of the most miserly ODI bowlers in the business, had trouble containing the Sri Lankans. Champion leggie Abdul Qadir was out injured so there wasn't a lot to turn to in the spin department, but Shoaib was brought in to the attack and got a superb ball through the dangerous Mahanama (35). Kuruppu continued to attack and received plenty of support from Aravinda de Silva who found his touch the moment he arrived at the crease.

However, the diminutive Shoaib deceived Kuruppu with his flight when the opener was on 60 and Yousuf completed the stumping. De Silva raced to 60 before being needlessly run out. Sri Lanka still had plenty of fight in them, but the game swung Pakistan's way.

Sound knocks by Arjuna (20), Mendis (10), Tillakaratne (10 not out) and Ratnayeke (18) helped take the Sri Lankans to a competitive 244.

It had been a long time since Pakistan's openers registered a half-century stand and again a poor start ensued when Rameez was bowled for five by a fine Ratnayake ball.

Shoaib, who bowled well, carried on the good form with the bat, making 65 before being bowled by Ratnayake who was back on for another spell. Amir Malik scored 20 before being bowled by Ashoka de Silva.

Pakistan did not need to overtake Sri Lanka's 244. As the teams played twice, Pakistan had a 30-run cushion from the first encounter. The Sri Lankan total in the second game meant Pakistan needed to make 215 runs in 50 overs to clinch the trophy, irrespective of the result.

Saleem Malik held the game in his capable hands. On the third ball of the 44th over, Malik flicked a ball from Ratnayake for a single and the title was Pakistan's. The match still carried on and Imran,

Imran Khan... all-time great

Abdul Qadir... leg-spin wizard

whose lusty hitting gave fans plenty to cheer, struck the winning runs in the 47th over and brought up his half century at the same time. Malik had some anxious moments on 99, but registered his ton with a regulation single. This gave the strike to Imran who didn't mess around, levelling the scores with two fours and winning the match with another boundary.

Malik was involved in two century partnerships. First, he added 102 with Shoaib for the third wicket with Shoaib's contribution 48 runs. Malik and his skipper each contributed 50 in the unfinished fourth-wicket stand.

CHAPTER 15

SUPREME SALEEM

Controversy and a tainted reputation still surrounds Saleem Malik, but at Test and one-day level he played many courageous and vital innings for his country. He could grind down an attack as he did for a Test series-levelling double century against the Australians or carve up the best bowlers in the world, irrespective of umpires, crowds, conditions or pitches.

Saleem Malik on the attack

Malik made a glorious 102 off 112 balls to spearhead Pakistan to a 38-run win over India in the deciding match of the Sharjah Champions Trophy in October 1989.

The victory gave Pakistan an unbeatable four-from-four record in the three-pronged (India, Pakistan, West Indies) tournament. India capitulated to Pakistan in this most vital of matches, but had the consolation of finishing runners-up because of a higher run-rate than the West Indies. India and West Indies had a win apiece.

Man-of-the-match and man-of-the-series, Malik was in brilliant touch against India in the last game, punching the ball to all points of the stadium to lift Pakistan to four for 252 in 47 overs. Malik, who struck five fours in his splendid ton, had already scored two half-centuries in the Champions Trophy and his aggregate for the four matches ended up 260.

Earlier, Imran led with bat and ball for a 57-run victory over the West Indies, the titleholders for the previous three years. It was an unusual contest because Javed Miandad, Wasim Akram, Viv Richards, Gus Logie and Malcolm Marshall watched the match from the stands due to injuries. And the West Indies were smarting from a surprise 37-run defeat by India. Pakistan beat West Indies by 11 runs in their first match and India by six wickets.

Imran won the toss and batted. His team was four for 86 but the captain whacked an unbeaten 60 from 57 balls to put Pakistan back on the rails. Curtley Ambrose and Ian Bishop refused to give the top order any leeway. After 50 overs Imran's team had knocked up 237 for the loss of seven wickets. Malik only scored 16.

The West Indies couldn't handle the guile of master spinner Abdul Qadir (10-1-31-3) or the blistering pace of exciting newcomer Waqar Younis (9-2-28-3).

Openers Phil Simmons and the champion Desmond Haynes guided the total to 43 in only nine overs, but both were dismissed when the explosive Waqar found an extra yard. The Caribbean side then slumped to five for 65. A lively 62-run partnership between Carlisle Best (44) and the gloveman Jeff Dujon (26) provided a glimmer of hope, but that's all it was.

There was stern stuff by the Pakistani bowlers in the game against India too as their attack was missing Imran Khan and Wasim Akram. However, Waqar Younis (6-0-18-0), Aquib Javed (10-0-49-3), Shahid Saeed (10-1-27-1), Mustaq Ahmed (6-0-32-2), Abdul

Qadir (7-0-35-0) and Shoaib Mohammed (8-0-42-2) made sure this game and the $35,000 first prize didn't get away.

Great Indian all-rounder Kapil Dev was also out, still troubled by a knee injury sustained against the West Indies earlier in the week.

Krishnamachari Srikkanth won the toss and asked Pakistan to bat. Without Kapil the attack looked decidedly lame. Malik was intent on making the most of life in the middle and all the Pakistani batsmen who visited the crease got among the runs.

Shahid Saeed went lbw to a Prabhakar yorker for 16, but fellow opener Shoaib settled in with Malik to put on 92 for the second wicket. Shoaib's 51 was his second half-century of the tournament

It's rare a one-day cricket match is won without some genuine batting fireworks and they came during the third-wicket stand between Malik and all-rounder Sohail Fazal, a newcomer to the top Pakistani XI.

Skipper Miandad, who had been plagued by a back injury and underwent extensive treatment in Lahore to get him on the plane to Sharjah, promoted Sohail up the order to crank up the run-rate. Sohail liked to break the ball, not just belt it! He obliged his skipper with 32 from 24 balls, including three thunderous sixes and a four.

Sohail savaged the usually economical Ravi Shastri with two sixes in a row, one that soared clean out of the stadium. A wag pointed out the ball had ice on it when it was eventually found. Sohail was caught Azhar off the bowling of Prabhakar. He passed his skipper at the pavilion gate with that satisfied spring in his step of a man who has done his job well. Miandad carried on the good work and was unbeaten on 28 after 47 overs.

Opener Srikkanth could destroy any attack in the world. India's hearts and hopes slumped when he was caught behind off Aquib Javed for eight. The next batsman in, the stylish Mohammed Azharuddin, was dismissed for 12 in a carbon copy of the dismissal of his captain.

Watching from the other end was opener Navjot Sidhu who played well, but he was soon snared by Mushtaq as the spinner gave more and more glimpses of the great career that lay before him.

Miandad applied more pressure. The bowling was tight, the fielding agile and slick. Dilip Vengsarkar grafted 35 from 73 balls, perhaps hoping someone could perform a miracle at the other end. Shastri cer-

tainly tried his best and while he was at the crease, which wasn't long, India still seemed in a match they hardly deserved to win.

Shastri faced 22 balls and scored 22 runs, making the job of tallying easy. The Indian all-rounder had been on the receiving end of some punishment when he bowled so he got some of his own back with a six off Mushtaq. But his next attempt at a big hit from Mushtaq resulted in holing out to Malik.

Ajay Sharma (6) was next to go, then Prabhakar was run out on 25. Mohinder Amarnath (30 not out) and Kiran More (21) threw the bat during the 'anything goes' overs, but it was a futile exercise.

Amarnath might have made a difference up the order, but he had been unwell and asked to bat at number eight instead of first drop.

Imran also cited other "incredible" one-day knocks by Malik, in Auckland, Trinidad and Calcutta, where the right-handed stroke-maker totally dominated world-class attacks. "Viv Richards would be proud of these innings," said Imran.

Aaqib Javed bowled well on a dead wicket and Sohail stepped on the gas at the right time. But this was Saleem Malik's game and series from the moment the wristy Lahore and Habib Bank player with the short backlift, deft touch and full range of strokes, took strike.Malik was man-of-the-match and man-of-the-series.

Imran Khan shares a joke with fast-bowling friend Malcolm Marshall. Cancer later claimed the life of the wonderful West Indian sportsman

CHAPTER 16

O'DONNELL SLAUGHTER REWRITES RECORD BOOKS

What a series!

The Sanyo Australasia Cup of mid-1990 had it all. There was sensational stroke-play, fierce pace bowling, mesmerising spin, hard-earned respect for the underdogs, gambles that paid off, hunches that didn't, and another hat-trick from Wasim Akram.

The left-arm fast bowler, battling injury and a fired-up Australian side, grabbed a hat-trick to clean up the tail and take Pakistan to victory in a wonderful tournament.

Simon O'Donnell hit the most ferocious 50 in one-day cricket history

But Akram's was one of only a number of the larger-than-life feats. Brave Simon O'Donnell, fit to play after triumphing over cancer, blasted the fastest half-century in one-day cricket history when he waded into Sri Lanka's bowlers.

Dean Jones was in superlative form, scoring 117 against Sri Lanka while Javed Miandad and David Boon were rock-like as ever. The tournament also saw Bangladesh take tentative steps on the world cricket stage.

The final. . . and that hat-trick. Akram sent Merv Hughes' leg stump into the air with the third ball of the 47th over. Carl Rackemann was bowled next ball, middle-and-leg. The crowd was baying for one more wicket. Akram, the most accurate new-ball bowler in world cricket, was too good for number 11 Terry Alderman, and the West Australian's stumps were scattered. This was brave stuff from Akram who had been troubled by a hamstring injury and a nosebleed.

The match against Allan Border's uncompromising charges was in the balance. Border's men played some sublime cricket to make it to the final and were highly competitive once in the tournament decider. Border opted for more bowling fire-power in the final, preferring fast bowler Hughes to steady opening batsman Geoff Marsh. As it turned out, Border could have done with the extra batsman and Hughes was particularly expensive at 10-0-55-0.

Pakistan scored 266 in the allotted 50 overs, the backbone of the innings being Saleem Malik, who made a chanceless 87 before falling to veteran spinner Peter Taylor, and Akram, who got 49 from only 35 balls. Akram's innings included three monstrous sixes and a four. Akram and Mushtaq put on 59 runs for an unbroken eighth wicket stand.

Australia kept getting a sniff of victory, such as when Javed went for 14, caught by wicketkeeper Ian Healy after he made an ordinary attempt to drive Steve Waugh. Imran also went cheaply, caught Healy off the bowling of the tall, blond fast bowler Rackemann. Healy took four catches on the day.

Pakistan were struggling at six for 179 in the 32nd over. Malik and Akram put on a quick-fire 28, but the cause looked far from hopeful when Malik was dismissed.

Australia's highly productive and uncompromising campaigners David Boon and Mark Taylor set about the task of catching Pakistan. They were off to a promising start of 62 before Boon was run out. Then

Waqar Younis exploded, clean bowling Jones for a duck and claiming Border lbw for one, both men beaten by the sheer pace of the young fast bowler. Younis finished the tournament with 17 wickets and the man-of-the-series title.

Australia were lifted by Steve Waugh, the man for the hard work even back in those youthful days, and O'Donnell, who had torn Sri Lanka to shreds.

Waugh (64) and O'Donnell (33) kept Australia well in the game until teenage spinner Mustaq Ahmed removed them both. Mustaq then picked up Peter Taylor for nine. Healy, not out 12, watched from the non-striker's end as Akram wrote himself another page in cricket history.

Imran said: "Akram turned the game around for us, first with his batting, then with his hat-trick. But we were a better team and after our score of 266 it was always going to be difficult for the Australians. On a flat wicket we are the best team in the world."

The road to the final was vintage stuff all the way.

David Boon, batting at four, pounded New Zealand for 92 not out to take the Aussies to 258 from 50 overs. Despite Martin Crowe being in the side (he scored 41), the Kiwis could muster only seven for 195 in reply. Australia looked like reaching 300 but New Zealand's gutsy fielding saved many runs.

Pakistan amassed 311 against Sri Lanka with Miandad (75) and Ejaz (89) the top scorers. The total topped the 294 against the West Indies in 1988. Ejaz, with eight fours and three sixes, was particularly savage on the Sri Lankans.

Younis, who took Sri Lanka apart, was fast and moved the ball late. He returned figures of six for 26. To pull off an unlikely victory Sri Lanka needed a big innings from Aravinda de Silva, but the Sri Lankan batting maestro was yorked for a duck by the best ball Younis bowled in the tournament. Thanks to Younis, Sri Lanka were bundled out for 221 in 47.4 overs, a crushing 90-run win to Pakistan.

Younis, with four scalps, was also the architect of the win over India. Pakistan set India 232, well within reach of such a talented side, but India fell 26 runs short with 24 balls remaining after a shocking collapse. Whenever India looked like putting a partnership together, Younis snuffed it out.

World champions Australia routed Bangladesh by seven wickets. Australia rested Alderman and Rackemann, but still had too much sting for the players from Bangladesh, who struggled to score eight for

134 in 50 overs after electing to bat first.

Sri Lanka were also heavily beaten by the in-form Aussies. Even Jones' innings of 117 not out seemed tame compared to O'Donnell's rampaging 74 which included the fastest 50 in one-day history anywhere in the world. The buccaneering Victorian's 50 came up in 18 balls, his 74 in 29 balls. O'Donnell put six sixes into the stunned crowd.

Australian Geoff Marsh played many fine innings in Sharjah before returning a decade later as coach of Zimbabwe

David Boon slashes through cover

Colourful Merv Hughes in action

O'Donnell's remarkable innings beat those of New Zealand's Lance Cairns and Pakistan's Saleem Malik who both hit half centuries in 21 balls. Cairns did it against Australia (1982-83) on the huge Melbourne Cricket Ground while Malik performed the feat against India at Calcutta's Eden Gardens. Australia's 332 (for the loss of three wickets) was their highest one-day score, eclipsing the two for 323 against Sri Lanka at the Adelaide Oval in 1984-85.

O'Donnell was a combination of beauty and anarchy. His first six was off Ratnayeke, on to the roof of the VIP stand. He quickly put another into the press box off the same bowler. Champaka Ramanayake was brought into the attack, but he was hit for 21 in his first over. Twenty came from O'Donnell's flashing

blade, including two more sixes, while Jones took a regulation single.

Sri Lanka chased well, especially Hashan Tillakaratne (76), but the ask was just too big.

More records tumbled when New Zealand also went on a run spree against enthusiastic newcomers Bangladesh. The small crowd cheered Bangladesh with gusto, but they needed wickets more than encouragement.

Openers Martin Crowe (69) and John Wright (93) and first drop Andrew Jones (93) pushed the Black Caps to a huge total of four for 338. Jones was brutal, his 93 coming off only 72 deliveries while Jones' innings included five fours and three sixes.

Opener Azhar Shantu did a great job against the Kiwi attack to compile 54 before losing his wicket to part-time bowler Ken Rutherford. Akram Khan hit 33 off 48 balls and Aminul Islam also used the long handle for an unconquered 30 off 41 deliveries. But Bangladesh scored only five for 177, which meant a 161-run win for New Zealand.

New Zealand's previous highest one-day total was five for 304, knocked up against Sri Lanka in Auckland in 1983. The opening stand by Crowe and Wright was another record, bettering the 152 by Glenn Turner and Bruce Edgar against England at Wellington, also in 1983. The 338 total briefly became the highest score ever at Sharjah, beating Pakistan's six for 294 against the West Indies in 1988.

When Mohammed Azharuddin made a magnificent 108 and Navjot Singh Sidhu scored an aggressive 64 to help India to 241, Sri Lanka looked all but gone.

By the 34th over Sri Lanka were six for 134 and six batsmen were out. But Arjuna Ranatunga was still there, like a Miandad, like a Boon, not knowing the meaning of backing down. He received plenty of willing support although no-one went on to a big score. But the target inched closer. Ranatunga slammed sixes off frontline Indian bowlers, Kapil, Prabhakar and Sharma.

In the 49th over, the burly skipper and Rumesh Ratnayake hit Prabhakar for 14 runs. Sri Lanka needed only five runs from the last over, which was bowled by Kapil. Rumesh got the runs with a four and a single. Another magnificent Sharjah cliff-hanger.

Sharjah dazzled with sparkling centuries by Azharuddin and Jones, true grit from Ranatunga and Miandad, Akram's hat-trick, pace like fire from Younis and O'Donnell hitting the most devastating ODI half-century ever.

CHAPTER 17

PAKISTAN POWER

Pakistan beat Sri Lanka by 50 runs to avenge defeat in the opening match of the 1990 Sharjah Instaphone Cup and win the tournament on superior run-rate. It won't go down as one of the best tournaments ever seen in Sharjah, but the two teams that turned up to play gave fans plenty of value.

India and the West Indies were invited, but pulled out. The West Indies decided to stay away due to the Gulf crisis following Iraq's invasion of Kuwait while India declined to play in Sharjah without offering an explanation.

When the two teams that did come settled down to play some cricket, veteran curator Mohammed Ishaq said the two pitches should produce a lot of runs. He added that only accurate medium pacers would pick up wickets, but that turned out to be only half-right. The medium pacers got among the wickets, but innings of three figures or thereabouts at this tournament were as rare as rained-off matches in the UAE.

Sri Lanka put Pakistan on the back foot in the first game, winning by six wickets in a stormy encounter marked by some controversial umpiring decisions. Bowler Rumesh Ratnayake and gloveman Heshan Tillakaratne had big games in a major upset against a team fresh from victories elsewhere against the Kiwis and West Indies. The win was even more praiseworthy because Akram and Younis were the most feared fast bowling attack in the world.

The Calypso cricketers danced to Ratnayeke's tune. Troubled by knee and ankle injuries and a hamstring strain, Ratnayake still took career-best one-day figures of five for 32.

Ratnayake was a fighting

cricketer who put considerable starch into his country's attack. He had a slingy action not unlike Jeff Thomson's and while obviously not as fast as 'Thommo' he generated real pace. He broke John Wright's nose with a bouncer, taking four for 81 in the second Test of that series in Wellington – then fainted at the sight of the blood! There would be no dispute about the Sri Lankan's pace from Larry Gomes of the West Indies, some of whose teeth were removed by a Ratnayake bouncer during the 1984-85 World Championship in Australia.

Pakistan conceded 44 extras, one run short of the top score by the opposition of 45 not out by the chunky little fighter Arjuna Ranatunga.

Ramanayake and Ratnayake made good use of the morning dew and general conditions. Their immacu-

Cooled things down... Javed Miandad

Pakistan's might was being felt 12 years later. Imran Nazir receives the Shell Helix Best Batsman award from Managing Director of Shell Pakistan Farooq Rahmatullah while the great Clive Lloyd looks on.

47

late line and length meant shots in front of the wicket were difficult top play, although

Pakistan started well enough with openers Saeed Anwar and Zahid Fazal putting on 46. A turning point was when Javed was run out for four to a lethal direct hit from Ramanayake. Then Ratnayake sent Pakistan from two for 56 to four for 57 with Zahid and Malik

Gritty... Arjuna Ranatunga

the men to go. Imran denied the hat-trick.

The numerous extras for no-balls and wides caused tempers to fray, especially after nine-ball overs by Akram and Anwar. Miandad managed to cool things down. Imran said later there were inconsistencies concerning wides and no-balls, but they "should not take away the essence of our defeat as we batted badly, fielded badly and bowled badly."

There wasn't much improvement in Pakistan the next game, but there was enough. Pakistan were rocked by Sri Lanka in the first match so a big win was needed second time around to ensure they took home the silverware and $20,000. The teams finished the tournament a win apiece but Pakistan's run rate was 4.08 per over against Sri Lanka's 3.65.

In vital game two a restrained, unbeaten 54 by man-of-the-match Ejaz Ahmed provided the bulk of Pakistan's total of 181 after they had lost three early wickets for 15 runs. He received solid support from Imran (30) and Aamir Suhail (32), who was making his international debut. Otherwise, Pakistan's much-vaunted batting line-up looked pretty ordinary, especially when Malik and Miandad went cheaply. Ejaz hit one six and one four in his steady 78-ball stay at the crease.

Sri Lanka showed zest and dynamism in the field and this was rewarded by four Pakistani batsmen being dismissed through run-outs.

Pakistan only managed to bat 43 overs for the loss of nine wickets. The total of 181 should have easy, especially as Sri Lanka were off to a good start when openers Dammika Ranatunga and Charat Senanayake shared a stand of 46.

Pakistan's spinners slowed the run rate. Sri Lanka lost four quick wickets for the addition of only 22 runs. Waqar Younis kept the pressure on with a spirited spell. A Younis thunderbolt blasted Aravinda de Silva's stumps out of the ground. Any chance Sri Lanka had of winning was clearly gone. Younis, bowling as fast as at any stage of his career, finished with three for 28 but leg spinner Mushtaq Ahmed, who also bowled magnificently to take three for 14, registered the best figures.

The match was a landmark for that formidable competitor Salim Yousuf, the Pakistani wicketkeeper. Yousuf registered his 100th victim in one-day internationals when he caught Senanayake off Akram Raza. Yousuf had also taken 100 dismissals in Tests and scored more than 1,000 runs.

CHAPTER 18

BEST OF THE BEST

"And the Man of the Match is Aaqib Javed . . ."

It sounds innocuous. We hear of match-winning accolades on each occasion this great game is played, but Aaqib Javed's legendary Sharjah effort will always be considered extraordinary.

Aaqib did more than beat India, he administered the last rites.

A bowler without fuss or showmanship and so often in the gigantic shadows of Imran Khan, Waqar Younis and Wasim Akram, Aaqib Javed had his day in the sun in the 1991 Wills Trophy final at Sharjah. Statistically, it was the greatest performance in one-day cricket history. As the Pakistani players clapped the journeyman bowler off the field the Indians pondered how one combative right-arm medium-pace bowler brought about their 72-run defeat.

Aaqib's seven for 37 was the best bowling analysis in a one-day international, eclipsing Winston Davis' seven for 50 against Australia in the 1983 World Cup. He even took a hat-trick. Not a bad trio either - Ravi Shastri, Mohammad Azharuddin and Sachin Tendulkar. They were amazing dismissals because all went lbw, playing across the line to one of the game's neatest, most efficient bowlers.

Azharuddin sent Pakistan in. After 12 overs both openers were out with only 25 runs on the board. But Saleem Malik exercised a steadying influence and was well supported by Zahid Fazal, only in the side because of injuries to regular members of the team, including Javed Miandad. The pair then stepped up the pace and put on a partnership of 171 runs. Malik's form was patchy leading up to this match, but he was at his elegant and commanding best in compiling 87 off 93 balls, an innings included six fours and a six. Zahid hit 98 in an innings of great character before cramp forced him to retire hurt.

Pakistan went to the break 262 for the loss of six wickets, a total within reach of the fine Indian batting line-up, particularly as earlier in the week they played sensational cricket to record their first win over Pakistan at Sharjah in six years. Pakistani looked to have the edge though.

India's early overs at the crease hinted at a close struggle. Sidhu was finding the middle of the bat. Imran went for 24 runs in four overs, but Akram bowled a wonderful spell of 6-3-8-0.

Imran threw the ball to Aaqib. His first dozen balls were accurate enough, but gave little indication of history in the making.

On the first ball of Aaqib's third over, with the score at 32 without loss, Moin Khan put down Shastri behind the stumps. One can only speculate on the outcome of the match had the 'keeper taken the catch. The next ball saw Shastri play across the line. He was given out lbw. Azharuddin and Tendulkar came and went in mirror images of Shastri. Four wickets fell before the total was 50. India batted aggressively but were always behind on the clock. With the scent of victory Pakistan moved in for the kill. Aaqib Javed led the way.

There was always a lingering feeling, however, that Pakistan would not taste victory until Kapil Dev was out and pretty soon he was. The bowler? Who else? Aaqib Javed.

Put in simple cricketing terms, Aaqib Javed, bowling on a tame wicket, drew a false shot from three world-class players who failed to find the ball with the bat. There was, of course, much more to it as Aaqib's name went into the record books for the hat-trick and the 'best-ever' analysis. India's batting line-up was a great one, but on October 25, 1991 Aaqib Javed, the man never considered a 'star', was greater.

Record haul... Aaqib Javed

CHAPTER 19

CREST OF GREATNESS

There was an almost palpable sense of something special about to happen as an unwavering Pakistan prepared for the Wills Trophy in the Sharjah nets in February 1993.

The team's commitment transcended this tournament. The players wanted to send a message to the cricket world at large, and they did. Pakistan had been routed on a disastrous tour of Australia and New Zealand when a great deal was expected of them, despite the absence of legendary Imran khan.

The Wills Trophy tournament featured an in-form Sri Lanka and Zimbabwe, no great shakes but improving all the time in international one-dayers.

A comment by Imran concerning Pakistan-Sri Lanka clashes seemed to surface every time the teams squared off: "If we beat Sri Lanka it's no big deal, but should we lose there will be hell to play back home." The quote did the rounds again and it definitely fired up Sri Lanka, but the only reaction in Pakistan following the tournament was jubilation. Pakistan, skippered by Wasim Akram, carved another monument to

Brilliant bowling...Wasim Akram

the country's dominance of Sharjah tournaments. The brief decline that started Down Under was arrested. Pakistan didn't just win, they achieved victory in grand style.

At Sharjah the pre-eminence of Wasim Akram had always been daunting, but now he was under a lot of pressure. Imran had retired and Akram was skipper, hand-picked by the great man who was devoting his attentions to a hospital for cancer sufferers.

If Imran was the Lion of Pakistan, Wasim was its tiger. He would prowl with the same menace as before he assumed the captaincy, but would he possess the tactical acumen of his illustrious predecessor

The warning out of Sharjah was ominous as records tumbled and Akram triumphed… and then some. Like Imran before him, Wasim Akram was formulating a legacy that would inspire another generation of players.

Arjuna Ranatunga did win the toss, but it wasn't Sri Lanka's day. Pakistan won the final against Sri Lanka by 114 runs. They slammed three for 283 and the demoralised Sri Lankans plodded to seven for 167.

Openers Saeed Anwar (110) and Rameez Raja (109 not out) steered Pakistan to the humiliation of their Asian rivals.

From the first few overs Anwar and Rameez looked set for big scores. Anwar took 62 balls to reach his half-century and 38 for the next 50 while Rameez hit his first 50 in 65 balls and his second in 44.

Ranatunga decided to slow the over rate and this led to a heated exchange with Rameez. But the Pakistanis in the pavilion, particularly Akram, didn't mind because only 41 of the 50 overs were bowled. Specialist bowlers Akram, Waqar Younis, Aaqib Javed and Mushtaq Ahmed would get their 10 overs, but the fifth – and non-specialist – only needed to bowl one. Ranatunga's tactics played into Akram's hands.

The hapless Sri Lankan bowling attack had no answer to the Pakistani openers. It wasn't until Anwar sliced a catch to gully that Sri Lanka had a little respite, although not a great deal. The left-handed batsman's 110 came off 104 balls with nine fours and a six, a vicious hit over extra cover from the bowling of Nishantha Ranatunga. Rameez remained unconquered on 109 to become his nation's leading ODI centurion. He had been equal on seven with icons Javed Miandad and Zaheer Abbas.

When Rameez and Anwar parted with the score on 204 they had bettered their own record for Pakistan by two runs, ironically set against Sri Lanka at the Adelaide Oval in 1989-90. It was also the highest partnership at the Sharjah ground, but the combative openers fell short of the 212 set by Australia's Geoff Marsh and David Boon against India at Jaipur in 1986-7.

Pakistan piled on the pressure. Inzamam belted 20 from 11 balls, Akram 22 off 11 balls and Javed scored 12 off the six balls he faced, including a savage straight drive for six.

Sri Lanka's openers Mahanama and Hathurusingha came out to bat to an asking rate of 6.87, another Sharjah record.

They say that if Mahanama bats well, Sri Lanka do well. A low, scorching ball from Akram trapped him in front of the wicket for a duck. Accurate … economical … able to vary his deliveries with great effect – that's Wasim Akram.

Aravinda de Silva is probably Sri Lanka's greatest batsman of all time. Graceful and a player of such crisp timing, de Silva's feats brought so many delights to fans in his cricket-loving country and all over the world. He needed a big score today and didn't get it. There were 15 runs on the board when Aaqib got him lbw for nine. There may have been a long way to go but it was all only a matter of time.

Hathurusingha and Gurusinga made a fight of it, but a controversial run out of the latter (36) seemed to unsettle his partner. Hathurusingha's (42) concentration lapsed and he chipped Aaqib's next ball to Mushtaq Ahmed at gully.

Ranatunga reckoned Gurusinga should have received the benefit of the doubt. Replays showed the umpire didn't appear in position and that the batsman seemed home. Ranatunga also felt Akram's confidence might have bluffed the umpire. The young captain was certainly learning!

Uncompromising Akram then successfully rapped the pads of Arjuna Ranatunga (25), Tillekeratne (11) and Nishantha Ranatunga (0), his second four-wicket haul of the tournament at a cost of a mere 24 runs. It earned him man-of-the-series honours. Anwar was man-of-the-match.

Pakistan qualified for the final by defeating Sri Lanka and Zimbabwe, while the Sri Lankans' victory over Zimbabwe got them through. Pakistan coasted to a 49-run win over a stout-hearted Zimbabwe. Inzamam's 90 (11 boundaries) was the mainstay of the 262 total and Akram's first victory as captain. Andy Flower (49) and brother Grant (57) led a spirited

charge but the rest of team couldn't keep it up.

Zimbabwe were unimpressive in chasing Sri Lanka's five for 266 in a rain-hit match, but brave lower-order player Eddo Andre Brandes unleashed some lusty hitting they still talk about in Emirates' cricket circles.

The tournament saw thunderstorms, a sandstorm, and now a one-man cyclone. Brandes hit the fastest half-century of the tournament – off 31 balls, with three sixes and three fours – to send a shudder up the collective Sri Lankan spine.

Zimbabwe were tottering at six for 85 off 23 overs when the no-frills tail-ender opened his shoulders. He put on 69 runs in 10 overs in the company of fellow tail-ender Ali Shah, then 40 in four overs with Gary Croker. The crowd roared underdog Brandes on throughout his brief but thrilling knock. He fell with the total at eight for 194 in 37.2 overs.

Brandes' 55 and two wickets won him man-of-the-match. Alas, he was not able to inspire an unlikely Zimbabwean victory, but he did take some of the shine from the Sri Lankan win, and all of the shine from the ball!

Aravinda de Silva is caught in two minds

CHAPTER 20

LARA: 'THE PRINCE AMONG BATSMEN'

From their effortless survival skills on a wet greentop to patience on a sun-caked piece of virtual tarmac, the West Indies can produce left-handed batsmen of such genius, flair and unpredictability they leave an indelible stamp on the game. Sir Garfield Sobers, Clive Lloyd, the late Roy Fredericks and Brian Lara - some of their innings transcended their generations and become hallmarks of the game.

The esoteric and sensitive Lara, nicknamed 'The Prince' by his friend Michael Whitney, scythed 150 magnificent runs to take the Champions Trophy final of November 1993 from Pakistan. Reflections of Sobers' classical 254 for the Rest of the World against Australia were seen from every regulation single through to each cleanly struck boundary.

The West Indies had the look of a squad that came to win. The star-studded side dominated Sri Lanka, the third team in the tournament. Pakistan, the world champions, were light on some quality personnel in the final.

The West Indies beat Pakistan by 31 runs in a match that gave the men in the red caps reason to feel good about the final. Pakistan blew away Sri Lanka's slender chances of a berth in the tournament decider by giving them 313 to chase in a key preliminary match. This was Pakistan's highest ever score in Sharjah, beating the 311, also against Sri Lanka, in 1990. Openers Saeed Anwar (107) and Asif Mujtaba (113 not out) got away well and Pakistan were never headed.

The final against a confident West Indies was a different matter. Chasing Pakistan's four for 284 off 50 overs, Lara, as he and only a couple of others of similarly exceptional talent can do, made the substantial target look neither here nor there.

There's no dispute Pakistan were weakened. No Wasim Akram, no Javed Miandad, no Aaqib Javed and no Abdul Qadir. There was Waqar Younis, but the big fast bowler from Multan, who was also handling captaincy duties, carried an injury.

The crowd had already seen one of one-day cricket's greatest innings, 127 by Basit Ali, scored in the blast furnace that only top cricketers know and the rest can simply imagine. The West Indies pace battery launched wave after wave of attack. Pakistan's top order fell away. After 28 overs Pakistan, asked to bat

by Richie Richardson, was in all sorts of trouble with three wickets gone and only 87 on the scoreboard.

Aamir Sohail (10) slashed the third ball of Kenny Benjamin's first over to Lara at first slip; classy fellow-

Brian Lara, the West Indian batting maestro

opener Saeed Anwar played on to Anderson Cummins and the always dangerous Inzamam fell for a Courtney Walsh three-card trick when he lofted the ball to Desmond Haynes at fine leg.

To put this remarkable match in some sort of context, the West Indies were 216 at the 30-over mark while Pakistan were 94 after the same number of overs.

Basit Ali followed the maxim, 'the best defence is attack' and in doing so became the second-fastest centurion in the history of one-day cricket. His 127 not out included five sixes and 12 fours. (The fastest ODI century is Mohammed Azharuddin's 100 off 62 balls versus New Zealand in India in 1989) Basit Ali's 100 came in 67 balls (four sixes and eight boundaries). His second 60 was willow mayhem, hit in only 25 balls.

Saleem Malik, realising his colleague was playing the innings of his career, farmed the strike ably. Yet Malik also stroked his way to 84 in 96 balls (one six, six fours) before being dismissed in the 49th over, caught Ambrose bowled Walsh. Basit Ali and Malik

were involved in a partnership of 172 runs.

As special as Basit Ali's firestorm had been, Lara extinguished it. Lara went after the bowling immediately and the century scored by this rare talent came in 96 balls, including 15 boundaries. Lara was so dominant he looked like he was having a net.

The experienced Haynes was out early, for three in the sixth over, off Mushtaq's bowling to a magnificent catch by 'keeper Rashid Latif who dived full length in front of first-slip area. Phil Simmons, later judged man of the series (he narrowly missed centuries in two preliminary round matches), ensured Lara received all necessary support.

It took the absolute best to dislodge Lara, a catch by Latif on the fly to his right that may well be the finest he ever took in first-class cricket. It was certainly the finest innings he ever terminated.

Sir Gary Sobers, the greatest all-round cricketer ever to play the game, is a supporter of Sharjah cricket as well as the efforts of his dynamic countryman, Lara

CHAPTER 21

WORLD BEATERS!

Aamir Sohail dominated the six-nation Australasia Cup series of 1994 and Inzamam ul-Haq produced one of his most explosive innings as Pakistan produced their absolute best to win the tournament.

Pakistan defeated India by 39 runs in the final to complete a hat-trick of Australasia Cup wins.

Pakistan went through to the final with a destruction of New Zealand that could have had the Kiwis calling for support from the UN. Number three batsman Inzamam and opener Sohail put on a slashing 263 runs in 251 balls, the highest partnership in the 23-year-history of one-day cricket. The dashing duo broke the record of 224, a third-wicket stand by Allan Border and Dean Jones against Sri Lanka in Adelaide in the 1984-5 season. The highest second-wicket stand

had been held by Viv Richards and Gordon Greenidge who scored 221 against India at Jamshedpur on the West Indies' 1983-4 tour.

Sohail was out (it shouldn't surprise, going for a big hit) for 134 and 'Inzy' carried his bat for 137. Pakistan batted out the 50 overs and finished two for 328, 10 short of the highest total ever scored at Sharjah. Ironically, the record belonged to New Zealand who scored four for 338 against Bangladesh during the 1989-90 season.

New Zealand chased well, especially Adam Parore who scored 82, but the winning total was always too far away.

India went through after accounting for Mark Taylor's Australians with a solid all-round display. The Aussies scored 244 with the main runs coming from Steve Waugh (53), Matt Hayden (48) and Justin Langer (36). The total wasn't easy to get because

Inzamam ul-Haq hits out in Sharjah

Taylor had at his disposal Glenn McGrath, Damien Fleming, Paul Reiffel and the mercurial Shane Warne.

McGrath versus Tendulkar … enough to whet the appetite of cricket lovers everywhere. McGrath won this one as Taylor held a fine catch at short mid-wicket to send the little champion back to the pavilion for only six. But Ajay Jadeja and Navjot Singh Sidhu held it all together, defending against the good balls - there were plenty of those - and caning the loose deliveries. They put on 131 off 172 balls, Jadeja scoring 87 and Sidhu 80 before both fell to Warne. India lost only three wickets in overtaking the Australian total in 45.4 overs.

But back to the final, and sensational Sohail.

Pakistan compiled 250 for the loss of six wickets. Sohail batted well for 69 and found good support in Saeed Anwar (47) and Basit Ali (57). Sohail showed such contempt for the bowling that he raced to 21 while his opening partner scored one run. Srinath gave away 32 in his first five overs, but he did clean bowl Sohail in his second spell when the man-of-the-series and man-of-the-match took a wild swing.

Pakistan seemed on course for another huge total, but lost the vital wickets of Inzamam (12) and Saleem Malik (1). Basit Ali got hold of the attack and ensured there would be no collapse. He hit Srinath for an amazing six over cover.

The 250 was 'gettable'. The run-rate graph showed that after 40 overs India were 180 whereas Pakistan had been 179, but India had lost two more wickets than their opponents.

India's top order squandered the chance of victory against the most accurate one-day bowlers in the world. Jadeja went for a duck in the first over, caught trying to pull Akram. India needed many more than 24 from Tendulkar and three from skipper

A copybook cover-drive by Steve Waugh

Azharuddin.

It wasn't until the fifth wicket that India really took the fight to Pakistan. The two left-handers, Vinod Kambli (56) and Atul Bedade (44), put on 80 runs in 101 balls. Bedade belted four sixes. However, the threat ended when Kambli drove Malik into the hands of Raz at short-mid-wicket. The Indians were all out for 211 in 47.4 overs.

Earlier in the tournament Pakistan accounted for India without much trouble although Tendulkar played beautifully for 73 off 61 balls. However, Saeed Anwar (72) and Basit Ali (75 not out) weren't to be outdone. India scored 219 in 46.3 overs, but Pakistan passed it in 44.3 overs for the loss of four wickets. Basit Ali sealed the match with a whopping six.

Sri Lanka flew into the UAE battered by a storm of controversy. Captain Arjuna Ranatunga and three players, as well as five selectors, quit in a furore over a fitness test for the tournament. Selectors retained 11 players from the previous 14-member team and picked four new ones to replace those who quit.

Five of the seven selectors also joined Ranatunga in resigning in a row over the fitness test that failed experienced batsman and vice-captain Aravinda de Silva and four others, including Ranatunga's brother. Fast bowler Pramodya Wickramasinghe, off-spinner Muttiah Muralidaran and opener Dulip Samaraweera then pulled out of the squad.

Many blamed Sports Minister Nanda Mathew for the crisis, but he refused to bow to the pressure and said: "We are a country of 17 million people. Even if all 14 players resign, we should be able to field a team."

Ranatunga, De Silva and the selectors said those conducting the fitness test were incompetent, but their demand for another fitness test was turned down.

Mahanama, a prolific opener who earlier replaced De Silva as vice-captain, was given Hashan Tillekeratne as his deputy. The captaincy was a touchy subject anyway, as Ranatunga was initially retained as captain despite criticism of his handling of a tour of India earlier in the year when Sri Lanka lost all three Tests by an innings.

The Sri Lankans didn't seem to have their minds on the game when they played Australia and scored only 155. Australia had little trouble with the total with Steve Waugh the most impressive with an 83-ball 64. All wasn't lost for Sri Lanka, but to go any further a big win over New Zealand was necessary.

Sri Lanka nearly pulled off a massive upset against the Kiwis. The spearhead was Asanka Gurusinha and the match was as exciting as any produced on this ground. Sri Lanka chased 217 and it came down to 10 runs needed off two balls. Gurusinha played one of the innings of his life and wasn't surrendering this game, especially after the strife before the players boarded the plane for the three-hour flight to the UAE.

Eight years ago, to the day, Javed Miandad won a match against India with a six off the last ball. Dion Nash, always accurate and hard to score off in tight situations like this, put the ball just about in the blockhole. Gurisinha sent it soaring over the bowler's head for six. The batsman swung wildly at the next ball, but it went to a fielder and resulted in only one run.

The Sri Lankans collapsed all through the order while the gritty opener defied the attack for 117 not out. There was no celebration from the centurion, who said: "We could have done it. It was a tough task, but we could have got it." At the end of the day the scorebook showed Sri Lanka needed 16 off the last over and got 13 of them. But Gurusinha's century was the first by a Sri Lankan at Sharjah and remains one of the best innings played there.

The Emirates Cricket Board side played with pluck and dignity throughout their first international tournament. Skipper Sultan Zarawani put India in when the two sides met and the total of 274 was too difficult. Mazhar Hussein batted steadily for 72 and Vijay Mehra was also sound in accumulating 43. The crowd was in raptures when Mazhar reached 50. But the home side found themselves in trouble trying to boost the run-rate. They needed 10 runs an over from the last 10 overs. The 202 ECB scored wasn't enough.

"Now we know the grey areas," said ECB coach Madan Lal.

India could have been forgiven if players' minds were not totally on the job as manager Ajit Wadekar, a stylish former Test skipper nicknamed 'Professor', suffered a heart attack on the morning of the match.

For the losing team, it was also a moment in history. "We lost to one of the best teams in the world," said captain Zarawani.

Pakistan walloped the UAE team by nine wickets, but the home team won a lot of praise for opting to bat first. The Emirates needed to score 290 and win the match to advance in the tournament. For the UAE side to even consider this showed wonderful spirit. But against Akram and co. more was required than willing spirit.

CHAPTER 22

AWESOME INDIA

India won the Asia Cup in Sharjah in April 1995, thanks to some delightful batting by skipper Mohammed Azharuddin (90 not out) and Navjot Singh Sidhu (84 not out) in the final against Sri Lanka, plus some Sachin Tendulkar magic in the lead-up matches.

It was a fitting farewell for the popular Ajit Wadekar who quit his manager's role with the Indian squad because of ill health.

Sri Lanka made the final after a five-wicket win over Pakistan saw Arjuna Ranatunga's men go through ahead of the Pakistanis on superior run-rate. Bangladesh also played in the tournament, but didn't rise to great heights.

Sri Lanka scored seven for 230 in 50 overs in the final, thanks mainly to Asanka Gurusinha's sheet-anchor innings of 85. The burly left-hander, who scored a fine century at the Sharjah ground 12 months earlier, was in total command and pulled his side out of a tight spot at four for 89.

Prabhakar went for nine but while Tendulkar was at the crease the game looked likely to be over in the blink of an eye. Tendulkar treated Chaminda Vaas and Champaka Ramanayke with contempt, playing shots all over the wicket for his 41 in 40 balls. This was Tendulkar at his greatest and a century looked as certain as these things can be, but he pulled Ramanayake from outside the off-stump and Jayasuriya lunged forward to take a great catch.

Tendulkar's exit saw Sidhu and Azharuddin together for an unbroken 173-run partnership in 184 balls. They took plenty of quick ones and twos and although they survived a couple of close calls for run-outs they guided India to a comfortable victory. India won the final by eight wickets with 7.1 overs in hand having maintained a scoring rate of five runs an over from the first ball. Ranatunga switched his bowlers and his fielders didn't give up, but the Indians were in command.

When Azharuddin's score ticked over to 48 he became the third batsman to score 1,000 runs in Sharjah, the other two being Pakistan's Javed Miandad and Saleem Malik.

India, and Tendulkar specifically, went into the final with a tremendous psychological advantage over Sri Lanka from the preliminary contest. India beat Sri Lanka by eight wickets in only 33.1 overs, Tendulkar blazing his way to an unbeaten 112. It was his fourth century in ODI cricket and it came off only 102 balls. The master batsman brought up 3,000 runs in the short game during this superb innings during which he struck 15 fours and a six.

But it was a different story when Sri Lanka took on Pakistan for what looked like a formality for the powerful Pakistani outfit. Sri Lanka chased a modest target of 179, but needed the runs in 33 overs to top Pakistan's run-rate and progress to the final. Sri Lanka changed their batting order with Roshan Mahanama promoted to open the innings and hold up the end for big-hitting Jayasuriya who brazenly cracked 30 in 15 balls.

N. S. Sidhu, one of the game's great characters

Sachin Tendulkar edges a ball through the slips... not the man to let off the hook

Aravinda de Silva, taking strike more than a foot outside the crease, was also savage on the attack with 23 in 27 balls. Mahanama swung the bat for 48 in 74 balls. Hashan Tillekaratne brought the win up with a six off spinner Arshad Khan in the 31st over. Sri Lanka needed to win in 33 overs and did it easily.

Top seamer Aaqib Javed was sorely missed. Officials said he withdrew from the match at the last minute because he "slipped in the bathroom".

Medium-pacer Aamir Nazir shared the new ball with Wasim Akram, but was caned by the Sri Lankans. His figures read: 5-0-47-1. The youngster was barely consolable at the end of the match. Welcome to the big league.

The victory in the final was India's 11th Cup triumph in international cricket and the fifth under Azharuddin. India's first Cup victory in international cricket was the 1983 World Cup triumph by the Kapil Dev-led side.

CHAPTER 23

LARA MAGNIFICENT, BUT R.I.P WINDIES

Sri Lanka wrote a poignant piece of history when they took the West Indies apart in the Singer Champions Trophy at Sharjah in October 1995, their first Cup win since receiving Test status in 1982. Many have followed, of course, including a World Cup triumph, but this was the first, it was special.

The West Indies had been in fine form all over the world and the majestic Brian Lara's run scoring seemed to know no bounds. Indeed, in this tournament, in a preliminary match, the left-hander had hit 169 off 129 balls against Sri Lanka. But the Windies didn't overawe Sri Lanka in Sharjah. West Indies scored 333 in the lead-up game, spurred by the Lara blitzkrieg, but brave Sri Lanka, five for 103 after 11.3 overs, came within a whisker of winning after a dynamic 100 from Hashan Tillekeratne. Fatigue caused him to vomit towards the end of his innings, but the determined Sri Lankan batsman kept on fighting.

This 'taster' for the final came down to the last over with Sri Lanka needing eight runs to win. Anderson Cummins had the ball in hand. Sri Lanka scored three. Tillekeratne whacked Cummins to square leg where Stuart Williams took a chest-high catch only a sprig mark in from the rope. That's how close this game was – and that's why Sri Lanka went into the final knowing that the first Cup title in history could soon be on its way to Colombo.

The West Indies of the 1980s could make heavy demands on the temperament of opponents. The future – and well-being – of batsmen depended on how well they coped against the speed men from the Caribbean. They were tough, they were persistent.

The mid-1990s was different. The windies' fast-bowling ranks lacked depth and Brian Lara - for all his genius with the bat - was prone to commit acts of indiscretion at the crease. Appeals against Richie Richardson were heard louder and more often than before. They were also more successful.

Sir Richard Hadlee was on record as tipping Sri Lanka to be the next World Cup champions. Few beyond the delightful beaches and majestic mountains of Sri Lanka took much notice. 'Sir Paddles' had seen a maturing Sri Lanka involved in some encounters that made opposing teams uneasy. He came away impressed.

Richardson won the toss in the final and elected to field. The decision raised a few eyebrows, since the West Indies weren't renowned chasers. They preferred to protect a total.

Sri Lanka were all out for 273 in their 50 overs. Richie Richardson's men fared poorly in the chase, all out for 223 in 47.3 overs.

Richie Richardson, the dignified captain of the West Indies

Lankan openers Rosh Mahanama and the indispensable Sanath Jayasuriya went out to build an innings. Fans' and teammates' confidence grew the longer they were there.

The West Indies attack wasn't too bad, but both batsmen were solid in defence and savage on anything loose. The West Indies missed Ian Bishop who had a leg injury. Anderson Cummins, Hamesh Anthony and Ottis Gibson were competitive but not of Bishop's fire and class.

Mahanama (66, off 103 balls - six fours) was named man-of-the-series and batsman-of-the-tournament. The innings of Jayasuriya (57, off 82 balls - five fours)

Arjuna Ranatunga.. tournament of triumph

Sanath Jayasuriya, Sri Lanka's competitve opening batsman

was also crucial.

Those with an eye on cricket's past and traditions can be been forgiven for thinking the gods of cricket had reincarnated Frank Wooley in a Sri Lankan cap when Jayasuriya is in form. He hit three sixes and each is worthy of comment. One was a brute of a shot over long-on from the bowling of spinner Shivnarine Chanderpaul. The others, off Phil Simmons, were all touch, technique and class. Jayasuriya used the pace of the ball well to pull two sixes over backward square leg and square leg, the latter landing on the road. It must be said that Simmons captured Jayasuriya's wicket the next ball as he tried to repeat the shot, but the batsman may have lost concentration as play was stopped for five minutes while the ball was found.

Aravinda de Silva turned the match into his personal picnic. He drove, cut and pulled with unrestrained ferocity. His 35-ball 50 included five fours and three sixes. Such was de Silva's confidence that he was walking down the wicket to meet the ball head-on, more often than not hitting through the line. Indeed, it was on such a stroll outside the crease that De Silva hit a memorable six. Simmons saw him coming and bowled the ball wide, but De Silva merely flashed the blade wide of his body and rolled his wrists. The ball sailed over cover.

Shivnarine Chanderpaul strokes a ball through cover at Sharjah Stadium

At two for 196, Sri Lanka looked like sailing past 300, but Anthony picked up the wickets of De Silva and Ranatunga. Roger Harper bowled a tight second spell. The Lankans lost eight wickets in the last 12 overs for 77 runs otherwise the total of 273 in 49.5 overs would have been much higher. Gibson bowled well, varying his pace nicely, and was rewarded with the figures of 5.5-0-35-4.

Sri Lanka were without strike bowler Pramodaya Wickramasinghe who sprained his ankle at the nets. His replacement, Eric Upashantha, 23, was not at all overawed, claiming the wickets of Stuart Williams (5) and the living legend Lara (8). Lara was totally out of sorts. For 25 balls he tried to find the gaps only to grow more frustrated. He was out offering the most simple of return catches as he tried to turn the ball to leg. There was no difficulty hearing the young bowler's appeal.

Upashantha and Hathurasinghe gave nothing away with only 57 runs coming off the first 15 overs. Sherwin Campbell (38 off 78 balls – two fours) did his best, but was unable to score freely.

The West Indies were unlikely to win the match, but things got even worse after two brilliant run-outs of danger men Richardson and Simmons. Richardson was dismissed via a direct hit from De Silva while Asanka Gurusinha got the ball in too quickly for Simmons. The run outs put the West Indies at four for 74 and they didn't fully recover.

Muralitharan ended the stubborn resistance of Campbell as well as Roger Harper (31 off 47 balls – two fours). Last-wicket pair Gibson (33 not out off 25 balls - three fours and a six) and Anthony (21 off 18 balls – two sixes) enjoyed themselves, but their big hits had no bearing on the result.

De Silva was man-of-the-match, Dhamramasena bowler-of the-tournament and Mahanama man-of-the-series and batsman-of-the-tournament.

Richardson said: "We lost to a very spirited team. They bowled, batted and fielded well. We did not. We deserved to lose. Hopefully I'll have learned a few lessons from this match as we prepare for the World Cup next year."

Ranatunga lifted the Champion's Trophy, Sri Lanka's first major silverware away from home, and remarked: "This is my finest moment with the team." It was Sri Lanka's fourth victory over the West Indies in 22 internationals, but the most important. It was also a glimpse, a clear glimpse, of things to come.

CHAPTER 24

KIRSTEN'S TONS... JUST FOR OPENERS

Gary Kirsten must love these couple of acres at Sharjah. The South African has scored a lot of runs in the emirate and his skills, unswerving commitment and desire were never in greater evidence than in the Pepsi Sharjah Cup in April 1996. The left-hander carried his bat for 155 runs to inspire a 38-run defeat of India in the final. It was the opener's second century against India during the tournament. The Indian team created history by beating Sharjah specialists Pakistan in the key qualifier.

South Africa's apartheid policy led to the cricket team's banishment from the international stage in 1970, the ban being lifted 20 years later when the Government's racist policies were consigned to history. It took a long time for South Africa to come to Sharjah, but Kirsten made it memorable when they did. He batted with a style to savour rather than unleashing a flurry of big hitting, leaving that to all-rounder Brian McMillan and the unlikely Pat Symcox, who was promoted up the order in the role of pinch hitter.

Hansie Cronje won the toss in the final and elected to bat. Kirsten, fresh from a regal ton against India only days before, went about the task at hand as though it were just a day at the office.

There was plenty to do as the Proteas were two for 20. Andrew Hudson actually went first ball for the second innings in a row. Kirsten looked steady rather than spectacular. Srinath and Prasad had trouble finding their respective lines as they strove for extra pace, but Kirsten was at times fencing outside off-stump.

Enter Symcox, best known as an economical off-spinner and sharp fielder. Cronje sent him in early to lift the tempo. Symcox, one of the coolest of players, possessed a keen eye and plenty of powerful strokes. He responded by hammering 61 off a mere 49 balls, including two sixes and five fours. The Kirsten-Symcox partnership was 95 off only 91 balls.

The giant, enigmatic all-rounder McMillan was next in and he spread the field with 37 off 24 balls, including three sixes and two fours. Spinner Venkatapathy must have been wondering what he did to deserve the final over when McMillan sent the last two balls of the innings into the crowd. This took South Africa to five for 287 in the designated 50 overs.

Vikram Rathore and Sachin Tendulkar strode down the steps on to the red carpet and out to the wicket. Tendulkar gave those characteristic little shrugs of his shoulders and tugs at his sleeves. Rathore and Tendulkar put on acceptable 59 in 13 overs, but chaos reigned in the middle order.

Tendulkar was on 57 when he was run out in a mix-up with Sidhu. Then Anil Kumble (10) was run out... and Sanjay Manjrekar (41)... and skipper Azharuddin (39).

Ian Chappell, Australia's former tough-as-teak captain, is a Sharjah regular in the capacity of commentator

Garry Kirsten limbers up in the nets at Sharjah

Hanse Cronje, South Africa's tragic captain

Panic yielded the four run-outs, but India nearly had to live with the ignominy of a world-record equalling five dismissals in this manner. Wicketkeeper Dave Richardson had the full face of three stumps to hit but failed to make contact when Srinath was well short of his ground.

Azharuddin did hit out, but the game was out of India's range against a side that could well have invented the term 'line-and-length'. Many felt the captain should have come in at number three instead of Sanjah Manjrekar and taken the fight to South Africa. It is significant that when Azharuddin looked dangerous - and there have been few faster between wickets - Symcox fired the bullet-like return from mid-wicket to hit the stumps and dismiss the Indian skipper.

This was not an epic tournament, but the clear victory by South Africa was further evidence that battle-hardened - although soon to be disgraced - Cronje and the team's mentor, Bob Woolmer, were fashioning an outstanding one-day side. Cronje was also propelling himself to shame and tragedy.

CHAPTER 25

RUNS AND RULES

Powerful Pakistan won the Champions Trophy of 1996, but a proud New Zealand must have wondered what might have been. Certainly the Kiwis could have batted a lot better in the final, but they did lose five batsmen lbw with three of those decisions difficult to understand.

And what of the Sri Lankans? After finishing level with New Zealand following the preliminary matches, they were told they'd be in the final, but match umpire Mike Smith (correctly) reversed his decision.

First up, the final.

New Zealand won the toss and asked Pakistan to have a bat. The Black Caps bowled tightly, fielded well and kept the pressure on, all good one-day stuff. Pakistan managed only 160 and it would have been considerably less if the usually safe hands of Nathan Astle had not spilled Saleem Malik early in his innings. Malik went on to top score with 40. Moin Khan hit out for 32, including three huge sixes, two of them in one over off Chris Harris.

The Kiwis were comfortable at 66 for the loss of one wicket, that of Brian Young, skittled early by as good a ball as Wasim Akram has ever bowled. Akram bowled superbly, but burly Mark Greatbatch handled him well. Greatbatch and Adam Parore also negotiated a sharp spell from Waqar Younis. Adam Parore was the Kiwis' anchor in earlier matches and wasn't going anywhere this time either, or so he thought. Saqlain Mushtaq rapped Parore on the pads and made the most half-hearted of appeals. Gone.

Pakistan pounced. A diving Mushtaq Ahmed caught Astle with the score on 81, and then Greatbatch top-edged a sweep to Ijaz Ahmed.

The batting needed resettling and Stephen Fleming, the composed left-hander, was the one who needed to do it. But Fleming jumped in the air to keep down a scorcher from Younis. The tall Fleming was hit on the pad above the knee roll. Gone.

Cairns and skipper Lee Germon fell lbw to Akram, and Patel the same way to Afridi. Germon clearly had cause to feel hard done by. New Zealand mustered 116, a dreadful score. Only Greatbatch and Parore entered double figures.

Germon wouldn't be drawn on the standard of umpiring (officiating were S.K. Bhansal , George Sharp and Ian Robinson) throughout the tournament.

He felt, however, that the New Zealand batsmen let down the bowlers. "It's not often we bowl out a team for 160. If you don't win from there, you don't deserve to win," said Germon.

Akram, man-of-the-match in the final (Younis was man-of-the-series), said: "Pakistan can never be taken lightly."

The three teams faced each other on two occasions with Pakistan winning all their matches to go through to the final. This included an eight-wicket mauling of Sri Lanka.

New Zealand lost the last of the league matches, a four-wicket defeat by Pakistan, meaning the Kiwis were on three points with Sri Lanka. (Earlier the teams figured in a tie when a spirited New Zealand bravely defended 169.) Tournament referee Smith announced

Chris Cairns, New Zealand's mighty all-rounder

the Sri Lankan side would advance to the final on superior run rate. However, shortly after the match Smith reversed his own decision after discussions with International Cricket Council chief Dave Richards.

Rule 11.1 states that if two teams have equal points, the side which has won more matches in the league goes through.

New Zealand beat Sri Lanka in one match and tied the other, so that seemed to indicate New Zealand should progress. Smith and some players were confused by parts of the wording of the rule, specifically where it said, "winner of all the preliminary match(es)."

The rule stated: "In the event of teams finishing on equal points, the right to play in the final will be decided by:

the most wins in the preliminary matches;
or when teams have both equal wins and equal points, the team which was the winner of all the preliminary match(es) played between them will be placed in a higher position;

or if still equal, the higher net run rate in the preliminary matches.

As players and fans awaited the verdict, many conversations centered on previous instances where the rule book caused major drama. A particular favourite was the rain-wrecked semi-final in the 1992 World Cup when South Africa, back on the international stage after two decades of isolation, required 22 runs from a single ball against England.

Ironically, the last word on this Sharjah encounter went to South Africa. The New Zealand management had dug in its heels. It sought clarification from the International Cricket Council, which in turn called the United Cricket Board of South Africa, which had, in fact, drafted the rules. The South African administrators conceded that the wording was ambiguous, but New Zealand had to be deemed finalists because they had the better league record against Sri Lanka.

Phew!

Pakistan always enjoys plenty of fan support at Sharjah

CHAPTER 26

ONE-DAY KINGS RETURN TO GLORY

Few sides have come to Sharjah to contest an 'off-shore' tournament with as much to prove as Sri Lanka did in April, 1997. Arjuna Ranatunga's charges unpacked their kit bags at the nets in Sharjah after a particularly miserable run. They won the Singer Cup at home, but lost multi-nation tournaments in remote outposts such as Singapore and Kenya. They were also beaten the previous year in Sharjah.

Form for this Singer Akai Cup looked to be Pakistan first, daylight second. Pakistan, skippered by Wasim Akram, were rated by an Indian computer-ranking system as the finest cricket team in the world - better than Australia and the West Indies - following the World Series victory a few months earlier.

Zimbabwe would have been easy-beats for the World Cup heroes even a year ago, but times had changed. Sri Lanka's current form was woeful while Zimbabwe stood up to be counted when they beat Mike Atherton's England in a home series of one-day-ers and narrowly missed the final of a triangular series against South Africa and India.

Sri Lanka's last campaign was in New Zealand where they were soundly beaten in both Tests and only managed to share the one-day series 1-1. Yet this team's showcase was adorned with the World Cup, snatched from the jaws of more fancied rivals only 13 months ago through a combination of explosive batting - particularly from the openers - dynamic fielding and tight bowling.

Duleep Mendis and Dav Whatmore, an Australian of Sri Lankan descent, who coached Sri Lanka to the

Dav Whatmore, Sri Lanka's astute coach

Muttiah Muralitharan... best bowler of the tounament

World Cup triumph, devised their revolutionary one-day batting strategy. The humiliating performances after the World Cup cost the burly former Victorian Test opening batsman his job. Fellow Australian Bruce Yardley, a former Test all-rounder nicknamed 'Roo', was the new coach. (Colombo-born Whatmore, who played seven Tests for Australia and scored more than 5,000 first-class runs for Victoria in the 1970s and 1980s is again coaching Sri Lanka.)

There was already a controversial backdrop to this Sharjah tournament. A furore erupted in Sri Lanka over the omission of highly competitive Asanka Gurusinha for the New Zealand and Sharjah tours. Duleep Mendis was stripped of his role of chief selector only a few days before the team arrived in Sharjah, although officials were at pains to say the sacking of Gurisinha did not figure in the equation.

However, Mendis and Ranatunga were particularly, some felt surprisingly, upbeat about the team's chances. "We're hoping to turn the wheel of fortune again," Mendis told reporters at the nets. "I'm certain we will bounce back." The poor showing in New Zealand made the team more determined to succeed in the $75,000 Sharjah tournament, the former Test captain said.

Ranatunga added: "The New Zealand tour is history now and the boys are pretty keen to take on Pakistan and Zimbabwe."

Their words were prophetic.

Batting maestro Aravinda de Silva dominated the tournament. His impeccable 87 off 124 balls powered Sri Lanka to their four-wicket win in the final, a tremendous match filled with last-gasp tension. Dashing De Silva's efforts in the final were only part of the tale as his scores in five innings totalled 410 runs at a staggering average of 136.66.

Sri Lanka beat Pakistan three times in this tournament and, in one of those victories De Silva played one of his finest ODI innings, that of 137 when he totally blitzed Akram's elite. It was Sri Lanka's first victory against Pakistan in a Cup final in Sharjah, a slice of history against all odds. De Silva was named man-of-the-final and man-of-the-series. Muttiah Muralitharan was best bower while Roshan Mahanama took the fielding honours.

The Sri Lankans were delayed 24 hours before returning home. When they set foot back on their island paradise it was secure in the knowledge they were again kings of the world of one-day cricket.

CHAPTER 27

SPY CHIEF'S RELATIVE IS ENGLAND'S SECRET WEAPON

Matthew Fleming, the great nephew of James Bond creator and war-time spy Ian Fleming, spearheaded a mighty victory over the West Indies in a classic Champions Trophy final in 1997. Indeed, storyteller Fleming could not have come up with a better cliff-hanger in which the underdog and hero won the day.

England were as good as beaten in this inaugural floodlit tournament in Sharjah. West Indies scored seven for 235, nothing special, but the Windies made any target difficult.

By the 41st over England had scored only 165 runs and six batsmen were given leave to shower. It looked like Thorpe might get a bit of batting practice before the Caribbean Kings hoisted the trophy aloft. Fleming was brought up the order by new skipper Adam Hollioake after a pow-wow with wily veteran Alec Stewart. Any chance of an England victory rested with runs being scored fast – starting now.

Fleming joined Thorpe in the middle. The revival started in over number 42 when Thorpe hit the first boundary for 15 run-starved overs. Fleming set about the West Indies bowlers, scoring 34 off 27 deliveries. England required 45 runs from six overs and won the game with two overs to spare. Sadly, Fleming was run out with the scores level, but it didn't seem to concern him. Fleming walked back to the pavilion - crossing with Dougie Brown, who whacked a four to seal the victory – with that unmistakable 'mission accomplished' strut. Man-of-the-match Thorpe remained unconquered on 66.

Earlier, West Indies skipper Courtney Walsh won the toss and elected to bat. The great fast bowler's

Carl Hooper can only look on as England celebrate the fall of another wicket

decision appeared to be vindicated when Shivnarine Chanderpaul and Stuart Williams put on an opening stand of 97 runs off 22 overs. The opening attack of Dean Headley and Dougie Brown didn't trouble the Windies openers at all and England looked in for a long afternoon and night in balmy Sharjah.

But, as they had done earlier in the week, Mark Ealam and Robert Croft cut back the scoring rate and grabbed vital wickets. Williams (56) was caught by Brown from Croft's bowling. Maestro Brian Lara was stumped by Stewart off Elam. Chanderpaul was run out to a brilliant throw from Fleming on a day when he could do no wrong.

The West Indies moved from cruise control to lower gear of three for 164 off 37 overs. Then Fleming struck. He picked up Carl Hooper (34), Roland Holder (0) and Franklyn Rose (0). Phil Simmons chipped in with 39 from 37 balls to minimise the damage.

England's start with the bat couldn't have been much worse with opener Ali Brown gone for one to the bowling of Rose. Nick Knight and Stewart put together a useful partnership and Stewart farewelled Walsh in his opening spell by hitting him for two boundaries.

Walsh introduced the spinners, Carl Hooper (orthodox) and Rawl Lewis (leggie) and runs were much harder to come by on a wearing deck.

Then came the collapse. Knight was run out (24), Graeme Hick played a poor shot off Lewis and was caught by Hooper for nine and a Hooper shooter bowled Stewart. Hollioake was stumped by Williams off Hooper for 16 and England were five for 152.

There was just one part of the script missing and it was striding to the wicket … Fleming.

Hollioake stressed that the tactical masterstroke to lift Fleming above the more sedate Dougie Brown was at Stewart's suggestion. "Some big hitting was needed at the time and Alec's view was that if Matthew made his shots it would certainly put us right back in it," the young captain, who had played just 10 one-day internationals, told the media.

"We thought if Matthew could get some quick runs Dougie could keep it going with the singles and twos, but it worked even better than we'd hoped. Alec made the suggestion and I had to make the decision. I'm pleased we did it that way."

An early start at Sharjah Stadium to get the wicket just right

CHAPTER 28

SACHIN'S SERIES

Time marches on, runs a cliché as well worn as a fifth-day strip at the Gadaffi Stadium in Lahore, but does it? Steve Waugh's Australians could have been forgiven for thinking, to coin another phrase, that time stood still.

The cricketing elite from the antipodes left India with their reputations - especially Shane Warne's – in tatters, mainly due to a Sachin Tendulkar thrashing of epic proportions.

It had all started with 204 not out for Mumbai at Brabourne Stadium. The Australians felt (or hoped) Tendulkar had peaked too early. But his single-minded determination, refusal to surrender his wicket cheaply and a fair chunk of natural ability, saw him pillage 446 runs in the three Tests, 123 more in a Pepsi Triangular that followed and, after that, 357 in three matches in Sharjah.

It was a batting avalanche that in two months saw Tendulkar score more than 1000 runs against Australia in all forms of cricket. The total over that period was 1130 in 10 matches with five centuries and the average a Bradman-esque 113.00.

The Australians wanted to answer their critics in the April 1998 Coca Cola Cup against India and New Zealand , but Tendulkar simply picked up where he left off a few hours plane ride away.

And if there was ever an omen... the India-Australia final was played on Tendulkar's 25th birthday.

New Zealand didn't have the best of tournaments. Stephen Fleming's men saved their best performance until last, against Australia, making five for 259 in 50 overs. Nathan Astle batted extremely well for 78 and Chris Cairns, who had an indifferent tournament, hit a fast 56. The Australians also lost five wickets in reaching the target, big Tom Moody leading the way with 63 and Michael Bevan, considered by many the most effective one-day batsman in the world, next best on 57.

Australia were in good nick, marching into the final on the back of three wins from as many matches. Despite Tendulkar's freakish form, the Indians were patchy. In the first preliminary game, India's 50th appearance in Sharjah, Australia scored 264 and India could reply with only 206, 80 of those from the slashing blade of Tendulkar. In the next match against the

Aussies he hit a scintillating 142 off just 131 balls. The diminutive genius plundered nine fours and five sixes, two of those in a row off big quick bowler Michael Kasprowicz. All this, and India didn't even win the game!

Bevan showed a wonderful repertoire of strokes in an innings of 101 not out. Mark Waugh, like Tendulkar, an open-

Sachin Tendulkar leaves the field after another Sharjah century

er in one-dayers, hit a typically stylish 81. India lost this match by 26 runs, failing to reach the revised target of 276 in 46 overs. The target was changed after a sandstorm blanketed the stadium in the 32nd over when India were four for 143.

New Zealand threw the series open with a hard-fought win over India. The Kiwis performed admirably to restrict India to 181, but struggled with the relatively easy chase. Craig McMillan's 53 was the cornerstone of the innings and subsequent win.

With India and the Kiwis at a win apiece, India automatically would go through to the final if they could manage a victory over Stephen Waugh's team. Without such a win, India would need to score 237 in 46 overs to qualify for the final. It was achieved in 42.5 overs, thanks to Tendulkar.

So to the final. . . Azharuddin won the toss and surprised everybody by sending the Aussies in. It seemed he would be vindicated. Australia lost three quick wickets and useful batsmen they were too – Mark Waugh, Ricky Ponting and Tom Moody. Moody was unlucky. India made only a half-hearted appeal for caught behind, but West Indian umpire Steve Bucknor answered in the affirmative. Repeated TV replays showed the ball missed the bottom edge of the bat. Bucknor did consult third umpire Ian Robinson as to whether 'keeper Nayan Mongia gloved the ball cleanly. Moody looked dangerous in scoring 39 off 35 balls with two fours and two sixes.

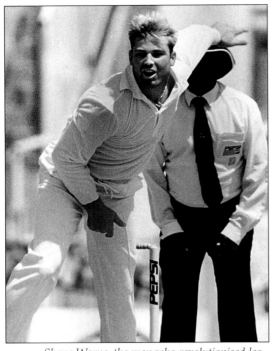

Shane Warne, the man who revolutionised leg-spin bowling.

Free-hitting Adam Gilchrist had forced his way into the one-day team while Ian Healy continued to be custodian of the Test arena. Gilchrist, the wicket-keeper batsman who went on to captain his country for the first time against the West Indies in December 2000, scored 45 from 60 balls – fairly moderate by his standards – before edging Hrishikesh Kanitkar through to Mongia. Gilchrist and Bevan (45 off 63 balls - two fours) put on 59 runs for the fourth wicket. Bevan was out when Steve Waugh failed to respond to his call for a second run. Both batsmen were stranded at one end. The Australians were five for 121 after 27 overs.

The Australian one-day captain and Test deputy did as he always does – fixed the bowlers with a steely stare and set about gaining control. Waugh ripped the Indian attack to pieces. Stocky Darren Lehman from Adelaide cranked up his own scoring rate as well. Lehman was especially savage square of the wicket. In 20 overs the pair were scoring at seven an over.

Lehman, who had just made his Test debut despite having scored more than 10,000 First Class runs, and Waugh more than arrested the decline, putting on 103 for the sixth wicket. Waugh was effortless in compiling 70 off 71 balls (four fours, one six) while Lehman's 70 came in only 59 balls and contained five fours and a six. Ironically, it was the first half-century innings by either player in the tournament. Waugh's Australians are nothing if not fighters and had actually been teetering on three for 26 after only 5.5 overs.

The Aussies finally set a target of 273, which was always going to be hard to get.

Pick of the Indian bowlers was Venkatesh who took two wickets for 32 runs and bowled with plenty of fire. He reached the landmark of 100 ODI wickets during the match.

So Tendulkar took strike as India prepared to respond. Perhaps he was not thinking about the fact that he came into this match having made 80 and 142 in the last two innings against Australia at this stadium in the desert. The master was unstoppable. Warne couldn't do a thing, the attack on the spinner an overflow of the merciless domination that occurred on the tour of India. To give Warne some due, he probably shouldn't have made the tour because of a nagging shoulder injury.

Chasing 273 under the Sharjah lights wasn't easy, but a few hours later the Indians were celebrating a six-wicket win over Australia.

Tendulkar exploded across the Emirates, scoring a breathtaking 134. Each time Tendulkar's blade struck, more records tumbled. He became the first Indian to score back-to-back centuries in one-day internationals. It was his fourth ton against the Australians in the shortened form of the game. Waugh later said Tendulkar would have to be rated the next-best batsman to Sir Donald Bradman. Tendulkar's 134 came in 131 balls and included 12 fours and three sixes. It was his 15th ODI century. It seemed improbable Tendulkar would ever get out and when it happened, lbw to the hard-working Kasprowicz, TV replays showed the ball going down leg side.

The wristy Azharuddin made an entertaining 58 off 64 balls. He also fell to Kasprowicz the next over and was annoyed to be given out, feeling the ball had clipped his pads. For the bowler they call 'Casper', it was fair reward for a lot of hard yards in the sun over the previous two months.

The 120 put on by Tendulkar and Azharuddin is India's best for the third wicket against Australia, beating 115 by Gavaskar and Shastri 14 years before. Tendulkar's 435 runs in five matches also set a new record for the most runs in a tournament other than a World Cup series or World Series Cricket in Australia, both of which comprised many more games.

In the 1997 Singer-Akai series in Sharjah Aravinda de Silva dominated as none before, belting 410 runs in five matches in a run-feast record that seemed likely to stand for years. The Sachin spree of April 1998 broke that record too. This was also India's first victory over Australia in a one-day tournament final. India had lost two World Series finals, in 1986 and 1991, and the final in Delhi only a month ago. There were to be no slip-ups in 'Sachin's Series'

CHAPTER 29

AKRAM'S TRUE GRIT

Plucky Wasim Akram left his sickbed to shatter India as Pakistan recorded an eight-wicket win in the final of the Coca Cola Cup of mid-1999. The great all-rounder, who had been running a high fever the previous night, unleashed a furious burst of pace bowling. Akram's thunderbolts sent India reeling early and they didn't recover.

India, skippered in the pool clashes by Ajay Jadeja due to a foot injury to Mohammed Azharuddin, won all three league matches in the tournament that also featured Alec Stewart's England. Pakistan started the tournament brilliantly, but lost the last two games before the final so they went into the decider in poor form and with Akram under a fitness cloud.

However, India didn't have a solitary run on the board in the final when Sadagopan Ramesh and Rahul Dravid were back in the dressing room taking off their pads, courtesy of Akram's opening burst. Both men went lbw and Akram was on a hat-trick. Akram had Azharuddin 'plumb' next ball but, with the team up in unison, all were greeted by the outstretched arm of Australian umpire Darryl Hair . . . signalling no-ball.

There wasn't much respite at the other end either as Shoaib Akhtar grabbed the wicket of Azharuddin (2), well caught at second slip by Azhar Mahmood.

Saurav Ganguly did his best to hold the fort, but India wilted. Ajit Agarkar (20) was second top score, but his teammates did not follow his lead in wagging the tail. Typical of Akram's efforts in this match, the fast bowler came back for a brief second spell and clean-bowled troublesome Agarkar. The last resistance was gone.

A few of the umpiring decisions didn't please the Indians, perhaps with some justification, but it was a batting display they'd rather put behind them. Akram's figures were an impressive 8-1-11-3, but they don't illustrate the venom he injected into those opening overs. His extraordinary first spell read, 7-3-8-2.

When Akram wasn't getting wickets the Indians were running themselves out. Robin Singh, Nayan Mongia and Anil Kumble all failed to make their ground.

Pakistan had no problems with the tiny target of 125. Saeed Anwar and Shahid Afridi effortlessly put on 53 before Afridi (24) lofted Anil Kumble to Ganguly at long-on. Anwar (30) followed only 12 runs later,

caught and bowled by Kumble. But the high-quality leg spinner would not be turning this match and Ijaz Ahmed (21 not out) and Inzamam ul-Haq (21 not out) walked off after 28 overs to join their teammates in claiming the trophy.

Shoaib Akhtar enjoys a soft drink between bowling blitzes

Akram was man-of-the-match, Akhtar bowler-of-the-tournament and player-of-the-tournament.

India were bundled out for 125 in Sharjah on another occasion, in 1985. They regrouped and won the match after firing out Imran Khan's Pakistani side for 87. Akram made sure lightning didn't strike twice.

England performed adequately at times, but not

Robin Singh cracks a ball through cover

when it really mattered. There was a good win over Pakistan then a gutsy display against India. In the first match against Pakistan, however, England were soundly defeated by 90 runs, Ijaz Ahmed scoring 137. There were some fine English moments for sure, such as the cracking 84 by Nick Knight against India and a well-drilled 79 by Graham Thorpe in the same match, but it didn't alter the fact that England's 230 couldn't

Shahid Afridi gets his eye in before the match

match their rivals' 239 and the loss put England out. They needed 17 runs off 10 balls with one wicket in hand. Darren Gough, who loves this sort of lower-order pressure, lofted Srinath for six over long-on to reduce the target to 11 from nine balls. But Gough made it easy for India in the end by trying to run a cheeky single with Angus Fraser and he didn't make it.

Alec Stewart was disappointed, but Azharuddin didn't have much to smile about a few days later in the final when Pakistan humiliated his team.

After the final Azharuddin said: "I don't know about all the talk about my way of leading the team compared to Ajay Jadeja's. All I know is that we did not play well today and we lost. Our batting collapsed and that was the only reason for the loss that I know. One hundred and twenty-five is not the kind of total you expect your bowlers to defend. Still, before going out to bat I quoted them the previous examples where a team faltered trying to get 125 runs. But Pakistan played sensibly and certainly better than us."

Akram was jubilant because he was particularly off-colour yet rose from his bed, and to the occasion. The win was the best tonic of all, he said. "I didn't sleep the entire night before this game and I was running a high temperature. But the need to perform in such an important game for my country spurred me on.

"I told you guys (the media) after our losses against England and India in the pool games that we were going to come back strongly. We won this tournament because we are the better side. Everybody in the team worked so hard and my hat is off to the youngsters who are coming up so well. We are enjoying our cricket and playing positively - that's why we win. What Imran and Javed used to teach me I'm applying now. And I am giving the same lessons to youngsters like Shoaib and Afridi."

Akram said it was too early to tip Pakistan for the World Cup. A long way away, Steve Waugh would have gone along with that.

Alex Stewart, one the most competitive players to wear the England colours

CHAPTER 30

UMPIRING MARS CUP TRIUMPH

It was all Pakistan again in the Sharjah Cup of October 1999, but the triumph by a side full of flair, confidence and talent was marred by some controversial umpiring decisions.

Pakistan set Sri Lanka only nine for 211 in the final. Pakistan's batting struggled against accurate Sri Lankan bowling and spirited fielding. Leggie Upul Chandana caused problems for all batsmen and finished with a three-wicket haul. Saeed Anwar (53) and Inzamam ul-Haq (54) kept the scoreboard ticking over, but there wasn't much in the way of support. No others in the Pakistani top order made double figures. Pakistan were in major strife at six for 148 in the 40th over but Akram belted 30 off 26 balls. The lower order put on 63 runs in the last 10 overs.

Aravinda de Silva and Romesh Kaluwitharana launched a murderous attack on the new ball to be one for 49 by the ninth over. The determined duo came together after the fourth-ball dismissal of Sanath Jayasuriya, who couldn't keep a short ball from Akram down and was caught in the gully by Shahid Afridi. However, within the space of one run both batsmen fell to what most neutral judges felt were extremely poor umpiring decisions. A collapse was triggered and Sri Lanka were all out for only 123.

Third umpire Steve Dunne of New Zealand ruled De Silva caught at first slip by Inzamam off the bowling of Razzaq. This was despite repeated TV replays showing the ball hit the ground before lodging between the fielder's knees. In fact, Dunne watched nearly a dozen replays of 'Inzy' grassing the chance.

De Silva, who hit four boundaries in his 25, was in tremendous form and had the Pakistani attack at his mercy. Coach Dav Whatmore was livid as De Silva walked back to the stands.

It didn't get any better. Kaluwitharana was unlucky to be ruled leg-before by England's David Shepherd in Wasim Akram's next

Sanath Jayasuriya... disappointed

over as the ball deflected from the bat on to the pad.

Their departure put Sri Lanka at three for 50. It soon became five for 66 as Azhar Mahmood had both Marvan Atapattu and Mahela Jayawardena caught behind. Mahmood bowled magnificently, finishing with five wickets for 28 following an even more impressive six for 18 in the previous match against the West Indies.

The Sri Lankan captain played down the umpiring errors, saying the team didn't bat well under pressure. Indeed, there was truth in that as well. Jayasuriya said: "We should have won after getting Pakistan out for such a low score."

Pakistan crushed the West Indies, the only other side in the Cup, by 138 runs in a match the Caribbean side had to win to advance to the final. The Windies were all out for 117 in 31.3 overs against Pakistan's five for 255.

Saeed Anwar lays the wood on

CHAPTER 31

WAQAR'S MILLENNIUM MAGIC

The world of cricket returned to Sharjah for the emirate's first international series of the new millennium. The media area was packed just as it was 19 years ago, but in April 2000 journalists did not have to fight over two Telex machines out the back. Some reporters now filed for online cricket publications starting with www.

But out in the middle it was business as usual, an intense triangular series featuring India, Pakistan and South Africa.

India had new skipper Saurav Ganguly feeling his way while Moin Khan had just taken the reins from Wasim Akram. Moin became Pakistan's 19th skipper in 20 years. There were no such leadership issues in the South African camp where Hanse Cronje was again at the helm - for the next two-and-a-half months.

Waqar Younis, victim of many disappointments throughout his career but still fiercely determined, claimed this series.

Waqar picked up his 300th wicket in one-day cricket when he trapped South Africa's Neil McKenzie lbw in a preliminary match. It was a special moment for the newly-wed speedster because he made his international debut at Sharjah. It was also at this ground, as a small child, that Younis watched Imran Khan and Javed Miandad establish Pakistan as a cricketing power of the '80s. Waqar, whose father worked in the emirate as an engineering contractor, came to Sharjah as an eight-year-old. "It was here (in Sharjah) I dreamt of being a fast bowler," he said, adding he would have reached the 300-wicket mark much earlier, but injuries and selection problems kept him out of the national side.

This looked to be South Africa's series, but Waqar Younis was having none of it.

The Proteas were getting it right most of the time and if they weren't, someone produced something special, always the hallmark of a good team. India were not playing up to par and Pakistan looked inconsistent. Things seemed decidedly 'iffy' when new coach Javed Miandad announced minutes before a match against South Africa that Akram and Shoaib Akhtar would not be in the team because both had sustained injuries. In fact, Aktar took the injury to the

Caribbean weeks later, but Akram was fit for the next match.

In the first preliminary match against South Africa, Pakistan unearthed an opening batsman of quality and potential in Imran Nazir, 18, who had played in the recent junior World Cup in Sri Lanka. His effortless 71 included three, hit crisply and straight. Younis Khan, batting at three, and who scored a Test century on

Waqar Younis joined the 300 club at the Sharjah ground where he watched matches as a child

Saurav Ganguly had a tough introduction as captain

Herschelle Gibbs puts some spin on

debut only two months before against Sri Lanka, chipped in with 48.

But South Africa extended their winning streak over Pakistan in one-day cricket to 14, with a three-wicket victory, when that colossus of the limited-overs game, Lance Klusener, grabbed four wickets in 11 balls.

Cronje's men came into this game on the back of a 10-wicket rout of India and were always specials to make the final. Makhaya Ntini put behind him a harrowing 20-month absence from international cricket in this Cup match. The 22-year-old fast bowler snared three for 36 in his first match back in South Africa's green strip. Ntini had recently been cleared of a rape charge in his home town of East London. He had not been considered for international duties since the Headingley Test against England in 1998. Ntini came to the Coca Cola Cup in Sharjah in place of champion speedster Allan Donald who went home after the Test series in India.

The Indian XI only scratched 164 (Shaun Pollock bowled the great Tendulkar for five). Openers Gary Kirsten (71 not out) and Herschelle Gibbs (87 not out) added insult to injury by reaching the modest target without any wickets falling.

Pakistan then lost to arch-rivals India by five-wickets. India made heavy weather of a modest target of 147, taking 43.3 overs to get home, mainly thanks to a pleasing 54 by Mohammed Azharuddin. It was difficult to fathom form in the double-leg preliminary rounds.

The final was a cracker. Moin won the toss and elected to bat. Fan-

favourite Akhtar was still out injured. Imran Nazir, dark-haired and lantern-jawed, stroked his way to 69, in doing so hoisting Shaun Pollock and Derek Crookes for sixes down the ground. Nazir misjudged the flight of a ball from Crookes and Mark Boucher completed a neat stumping. If Nazir was elegant, Shahid Afridi was ultra-aggressive in his 52.

Inzamam ul-Haq, in good form with the bat after peeling off a remarkable and powerful century against India a week earlier (South African great Barry

Mohammed Azharuddin skies a ball

Mark Boucher at practice with an unusual stump

South African fans are a loyal lot

Jacques Kallis sends one down

Richards said it was one the finest innings he had seen in Sharjah), anchored the middle order with 53. After 50 overs Pakistan came up with six for 263. A lesser fielding side would have been chasing 300-plus.

Akram broke through early, Inzamam in slips holding a screamer from Gibbs.

Cronje accepted the challenge with a fine captain's knock. There was flair, ferocity and plenty of grit in his 79. He swung spinner Arshad Khan for a big six over mid-wicket, but in trying to repeat the exercise, holed out in the deep. It was seemingly a soft dismissal and it came under scrutiny months later when Cronje's career went under the microscope. The six was also the last scoring shot the enigmatic man played in international cricket. Several months later Cronje was banned for life over accepting money from bookmakers. Two years later the God-fearing man who was rebuilding his troubled life saw the great umpire in the sky raise his finger and Cronje died in a plane crash.

But Boucher was using the long handle and opener Neil McKenzie, who dropped anchor early, was still there. Big hitters Klusener and Pollock lurked ominously in the stands.

Waqar asked for a second-spell shot from Akram's preferred pavilion end. Boucher, 57, was in good touch, but Waqar clean bowled him. The ball was too fast and the batsman misjudged the line.

Nicky Boje was gone minutes later, Moin accepting the catch from a Waqar lifter on the deadest of wickets. With the South African section of the crowd chanting "Zulu, Zulu", Lance Klusener, the world's top one-day pinch-hitter, took guard. He was too late jamming the bat down as the three stumps were scattered by a yorker from Younis. A flicker of hope remained while Pollock was at the crease, but he, too, was bowled - on 14, all ends up - by another devastating Waqar Younis yorker.

So often statistics don't reveal all. Younis had, in fact, been relatively expensive at 10-0-62-4, but the ferocity of his second spell turned the match. The man once hailed as the world's fastest bowler said he'd sacrificed a "bit of pace" for guile. Perhaps, but he was still swift.

"It's all been a challenge," he said. "But I never give up."

And with that Waqar Younis accepted the awards for most wickets of the series, man-of-the-series and man-of-the-match.

CHAPTER 32

SANATH SLAYS INDIA, FLOWER BLOOMS IN DESERT

Sanath Jayasuriya, the gifted yet undemonstrative little Sri Lankan left-hander, turned the calendar to 20 years of limited-over internationals in Sharjah with a one-man demolition of India. Has there ever been a greater one-day innings than his blazing 189 off 161 balls (21 fours and four sixes) against India in the final of the Coca-Cola Trophy?

Well, yes, there have, that's for sure. Clive Lloyd's ton against in the first World Cup final at Lord's in 1975, Steve Waugh's century against South Africa in 1999 World Cup to take his team through to the final, which they won. Kapil Dev's century deluxe of 175 not out after coming in at Tunbridge Wells when India were four for 10 and seeing them decline to seven for 78. He got his little-considered team through to the World Cup final at Lord's and 'Kapil's Devils' beat the West Indies. In Sharjah, there had already been Miandad's six off the last ball . . . .

Sri Lanka looked good all through the two weeks of league matches in this Sharjah tournament. The third team in the triangular series, Zimbabwe, had burly former Australian Test fast bowler Carl Rackemann handling coaching duties. The Queenslander was appointed three weeks before the tournament. Andy Flower, in particular, was in impeccable form with the bat and Zimbabwe were unlucky not to play in the final.

As for India, well, Sharjah is virtually a home game. There's no respite for any side in the cauldron that is Sharjah when India is in a final, especially while Tendulkar is at the crease. Others enter at their emotional and, when batting, physical peril.

Sri Lanka impressed in the tournament, especially skipper Jayasuriya. His 87 against Zimbabwe deserved a century, but he moved too far across to the off and exposed his leg stump.

But Jayasuriya, short and sturdy, had improved his technique a great deal in recent years without sacrificing any of his exhilarating aggression. It was in that frame of mind that he went out to bat in the final intent on collaring India, and succeeded brilliantly.

It is said the true stamp of greatness is seen on players who produce their absolute best, the big innings, the match-winning hauls of wickets, when it really matters, when the pressure is right on. They have a different mindset. Sanath Jayasuriya is such a player. He was like a champion fighter coming out of the corner as he jabbed, parried and fired combinations. Once on top he was ruthless, hitting harder and harder. Unrelenting pressure.

The Indian players didn't want to know when it was their turn at the crease. Again, the boxing analogy – Ganguly's men threw in the towel.

It looked like Jayasuriya would be the first man to hit a double century in a limited-overs international. His blistering 189 was the highest score ever made at Sharjah, beating Brian Lara's 161. He fell agonisingly short of Saeed Anwar's world record 194, but drew level with master-blaster Viv Richards for the second-highest one-day knock of all time.

This was a special innings from the Sri Lankan captain, history being written and rewritten as the ball found the boundary advertising hoardings time and again. Arnold ensured the magic didn't end by a run-out. The pair put on 166 in 124 balls. Russell Arnold was a rock through most of it, finding the gaps, work-

Andy Flower whips a ball to leg

77

ing the singles, getting the calls right.

Sri Lanka's fielders strode out to bowl and field under the lights on this Sharjah night, having set india 299 scored for the loss of only five wickets. India's fans hoped Sri Lanka's bowlers would have trouble with the wet ball. It had been an extremely humid week which left a lot of dew on the ground in the evening. But for two days, light shamals (breezes) blew through the emirate. Sri Lanka's astute coach Dav Whatmore felt the ball would not be as wet as in the previous week.

Yuvraj Singh... painted as a player of the future

The pro-India crowd roared on their heroes but Sri Lankan paceman Chaminda Vaas paid no heed. Saurav Ganguly, who had a tournament he'd rather forget, went cheaply, again attempting a big hit. Sachin Tendulkar miscued an uncharacteristic wild swipe and the appeal was loud enough to be heard back in the great batsman's home town of Mumbai.

Tendulkar had already produced a workmanlike century against Sri Lanka in the opening league game on a sleepy wicket which made free-flowing scoring difficult.

This could have been 'the' moment for Yuvraj Singh, the charismatic teenager with the out-and-out quality of a budding superstar written all over him. He makes full use of the crease, hits the ball so cleanly and, his fielding is nothing short of brilliant. A final, a crisis, a crowd. But Singh couldn't transform this game, holing out early with a poor shot. Vinod Kambli had been in poor form and he remained in his slump when he became the fourth victim of Vaas.

No team this tournament handled Muttiah Muralitharan and he ripped through the tail in the final. The lively spinner had already set the world record for best ODI bowling performance when he took seven Indian wickets for 30 in the last league match before the final. His feat beat Aaqib Javed's seven wickets for 37 against India in Sharjah in 1991-2. Muralitharan also became the first Sri Lankan, and the 12th bowler, to take 200 wickets in international limited-overs cricket. The jaunty spinner's three wickets for six runs prevented any rearguard action by India. Only Robin Singh made it to double figures.

India were all out for an ignominious 54, trounced by 245 runs.

There were so many more records here to keep the statisticians busy after close of play but the one that mattered, unfortunately for India, was that this was the lowest score ever by an Indian team. This spanned 454 matches at home and at all points of the globe. The

Sanath Jayasuriya... record-breaking knock

Stretching time for Zimbabwe

worst previous outing was 63 against Australia at the Sydney Cricket Ground in 1991.

It got worse. The 245-run margin of victory by Sri Lanka eclipsed the previous best, 233 by Pakistan over Bangladesh in the Asia Cup in Dhaka earlier in 2000.

Bizarre as it might seem, Sri Lanka didn't have the match all their own way. India stemmed the flow of Sri Lankan runs at about the 28th over when their opponents were four for 116. 'Keeper-batsman Romesh Kaluwitharana looked dangerous, but he was dismissed and India's spinners, Tendulkar and Sunil Joshi, were proving hard to get away. The spinners grabbed the wickets of Marvan Atapattu, Mahela Jayawardene and Kumar Sangakkara. At over number 30 the score was four for 124. However, Arnold came to the fore, permitting Jayasuriya to set about removing the spine from India's bowling attack. Arnold had no difficulty playing the spinners and although overshadowed by Jayasuriya's hurricane knock, still cracked 52 off 62 balls, including two fours and a six.

Jayasuriya was given a life at 93 when Joshi spilled a caught-and-bowled opportunity. He'll have nightmares about that one for a long time. The Sri Lankan captain put the temporary lapse behind him and completed his century in 118 balls (10 fours, one six). His 150 took 143 balls (16 fours, three sixes).

It must have taken a lot for the despondent Ganguly to front up to the post-final press conference. His own form was a problem and he had presided over the worst ODI performance in the history of arguably the proudest of cricketing nations.

"I've got no excuses for this performance and no explanations," he said. "I know it's a sad day for all the Indian supporters here in Sharjah and back home in India. The boys should have realised what to do when we lost a few early wickets. We should have tried to stay at the wicket to see it through to the 50 overs. However, all credit must go to Sri Lanka, especially Sanath Jayasuriya who took the game away

from us."

There are few more modest or humble men across the spectrum of cricket than Jayasuriya. He had played one of the limited-over game's greatest innings, yet he only chose to say: "Our bowling won us the tournament. We came to Sharjah early to train and get acclimatised as the weather in Sri Lanka wasn't conducive to training. In the final, credit goes to the whole team, especially Vass and Muralitharan for their efforts with the ball, and Russell Arnold who supported me in the middle."

What about that world record for highest individual score? Was it a factor?

"No, I wasn't looking at the world record at all. My target was to post 300 and win the game."

After Jayasuriya's heroics in the final it is easy to forget the league fixtures that took the teams there, but there was some absorbing cricket over this special fortnight.

Sri Lanka drew first blood, needing only 43.5 overs to catch India's total of 224 for the loss of eight wickets. The slow pitch made it difficult for Tendulkar, but he still put together a 'routine' 101, his 26th century and seventh at Sharjah. Anishka Gunawardenaz dropped a 'sitter' at midwicket when Tendulkar was on 26. He was the only fieldsman for miles and the little man with the giant blade picked him out. It didn't happen again. Three top-order run-outs were an early indication that the Indian players didn't have their minds on the job. Finals heroes Jayasuriya (48) and Arnold (59) were the pick of the Sri Lankan bastmen in this match as well.

Sri Lanka passed Zimbabwe's total of 225 with 18

The champion Sri Lankan team

It was a tournament Ganguly will want to forget

Muttiah Muralitharan prepares to weave his spell

balls to spare in a superb match full of all those twists and turns that make cricket such a wonderful game. Of Zimbabwe's 225, 120 not out came from the bat of Andy Flower, and what a knock it was.

Muttiah Muralitharan made Zimbabwe earn every run. Zimbabwean wickets (four for 72) were falling like the proverbial nine-pins but Flower displayed every shot in the book and a few more to boot. He played three successful reverse sweeps in one over against Muralitharan and used the reverse sweep twice in another over for boundaries from the off-spinner on both occasions. Flower's only six was a big thump over mid-wicket from the bowling of Jayasuriya. Dirk Viljoen hit out and was unconquered on 63.

Flower, the rhythmic left-hander, became the first Zimbabwean batsman to post a three-figure score in Sharjah. He had held the previous record for highest score (95) by a batsman from his country in Sharjah which he made against Sri Lanka in 1998. And Flower and Viljoen put on 153 runs for their unbroken fifth wicket partnership against the Sri Lankans, a new record for Zimbabwe in ODI cricket.

Great stuff from Zimbabwe, but Sri Lanka's extra bit of class told on the day.

Sri Lanka ended the league phase with Muttiah delivering a world-record performance against India. Given the wisdom of hindsight, India never recovered from this psychological mauling. The spinner with the twisted forearm and exceptional powers of spin snared seven wickets for only 30 runs. The scalps weren't too bad either: Robin Singh, Sachin Tendulkar, Yuvraj Singh, Vinod Kambli, Hemang Badani and Sunil Joshi. He bowled after a Sri Lankan run riot of five for 294 with centuries by Kaluwitharana (128 off 121 balls) and Atapattu (102 off 111 balls).

India, two wickets down and only 24 on the board were always in the hunt while Tendulkar was in full flow and he reached 61 from 53 balls before Muttiah struck.

Whatmore, the brains behind the 1996 World Cup triumph, now in his second contract with Sri Lanka, did it again. (Whatmore had a stint coaching English country Warwickshire before agreeing to another appointment in Colombo.) Sri Lanka won all four league matches before crushing India in the final. The squad would head to South Africa in two months with plenty of confidence for a tour comprising three Tests and five one-dayers.

Whatmore said: "We're continually striving to be one of the best Test and one-day cricket nations. We want to be known as fearsome opponents, highly competitive wherever we play. We take matches one game at a time, but we're always trying to develop new talent and we always have our eye on the future. We're not getting carried away with these wins, but we came to do a job and we did it. We arrived early to train and everyone remained focused. In terms of consistency, I don't think I've seen Sri Lanka perform better."

And Jayasuriya's knock?

"It was one of the greatest innings I've ever seen. Everyone here at the ground was privileged to see this wonderful batsman display his wares. You just don't see batting like that every day of the week. It was a truly wonderful innings. I was willing him on to the world record, but it wasn't to be."

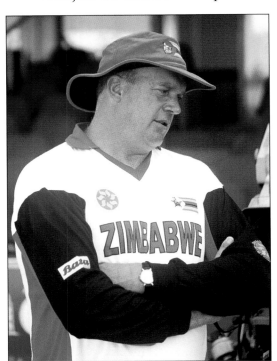

Australian bowler Carl Rackemann in Sharjah during his stint as coach of Zimbabwe

CHAPTER 33

INDIA OUT!

As Gulf cricket fans geared up for the 20th anniversary tournament in Sharjah featuring arch-rival sub-continent sides India, Pakistan and Sri Lanka, the unthinkable happened ... India pulled out.

India shut the door on Sharjah cricket for three years. At the time of going to press there has not been any significant breakthrough in getting India to return to the Sharjah fold.

With the players virtually packing their kit-bags for the Gulf, the Indian Government announced it had denied permission to its cricket team to play in the limited-overs tri-series.

An official release from the sports ministry said India would keep away from "non-regular venues" like Sharjah, Singapore and Toronto for the next three years.

"The Government has decided, after careful consideration, that the Indian cricket team should not participate in cricket tournaments at non-regular venues such as Sharjah, Singapore, Toronto etc. for at least three years.

"The Board of Control for Cricket (BCCI) in India has accordingly been informed that the Indian cricket team should not participate in the forthcoming tournament in Sharjah commencing April 8, 2001," the statement said.

Sources said at the time the Indian Government was wary of the national team taking part in offshore limited-overs series in the wake of the match-fixing scandal that had rocked the sport.

The scandal had just seen life bans imposed on three former captains: Cronje of South Africa, Azharuddin of India and Malik of Pakistan. Three other Indian players – Ajay Jadeja, Manoj Prabhakar and Ajay Sharma - who were charged by federal investigators over having links with bookmakers, were also penalised.

The CBFS official response was:

"Today, April 1, 2001, the CBFS has been informed by the BCCI that the Indian Government has refused permission for the Indian team to participate in the triangular series between India, Pakistan and Sri Lanka scheduled April 8-20.

"We regret that the Government of India has made this decision. The CBFS would like to thank the BCCI for their support and understand their impediment

The sign was premature

due to this unusual breach of contract forced upon them.

"We are confident that this discriminatory and unwarranted treatment of the Emirates Cricket Board will not be allowed to continue and the Government of India will reverse their decision in the near future." (India and Pakistan are signatories to a three-year contract with the CBFS that Sharjah's cricket authorities say binds them to play each other in Sharjah at least once a year.)

The statement went on that New Zealand had been roped in as the third team of the tournament, which would go ahead on schedule "and cricket in Sharjah will flourish as usual."

However, a bitterly disappointed Bukhatir flew to New Delhi in an attempt to ascertain the reasons for India's withdrawal.

He told reporters in India: "With less than a fortnight to go for the tournament, no-one has told us why India will not play in Sharjah. The UAE ambassador to India accompanied me to meet foreign ministry officials, but we were not given any reason for the Indian Government's decision.

"If it is because of Pakistan's participation, we will accept that because it is a political thing and we can't do anything about it. But, if it's about Sharjah, as some reports suggest, we have a right to know the reason. It is not fair to keep us in the dark about something that concerns us directly.

When would Tendulkar's genius return to Sharjah?

"Our ambassador kept asking (foreign ministry officials) what the problem was, but he got no reply. "

Bukhatir said it was unfair to accuse the CBFS of links with match-fixing or book-makers. "If investigations show that some games have been fixed in certain parts of the world, the organisers cannot be blamed. They should catch the book-ies or the players who are the culprits."

Bukhatir also pointed out that the CBFS had launched its own investigation to find out if any matches in Sharjah had been fixed. The three-member probe committee included former West Indian captain Clive Lloyd. The CBFS was awaiting the findings, he said.

Jawawant Lele, secretary of the BCCI, said the matter was out the organisa-tion's hands. "It has to be understood that the decision not to go to Sharjah was taken by the Government and not by cricket officials. The board cannot go against the wishes of the Government."

An official comment was not forthcom-ing from Uma Bharti, India's sports min-ister, until the tournament was well under way. She said India had no prob-lems with its team playing in Sharjah, but the Government did not want the side to play against Pakistan due to heightened tensions over the disputed territory of Kashmir.

"Before taking the decision not to play Pakistan, many people were consulted, including some players and officials," she said.

Bharti was asked why the cricket teams were precluded from playing when India and Pakistan competed on the field in other sports. She replied: "In India cricket has become the expression of national sentiments."

Bukhatir was as diplomatic as ever. "I am pleased that finally the Indian sports minister has cleared the doubts. I am happy that the excellent bilateral rela-tions that the UAE shares with India have been acknowledged."

CHAPTER 34

THE GAME GOES ON ...

A determined display by Sri Lanka condemned Pakistan to defeat in the final of the historic 20th anniversary tournament after the Pakistanis dominated the preliminary matches.

Pakistan won each of their four matches while Sri Lanka managed a lone victory, over an under-strength New Zealand. The Kiwis beat Sri Lanka as well, in the last pool match, but Sri Lanka progressed to the final on percentages.

Sri Lanka scored seven for 297 in the allotted 50 overs in the final. Pakistan were all out for 220 in 41.4 overs.

But the man most fans were talking about as the Sri Lankans did their lap of honour with the ARY Gold Cup, did not even play in the final.

Kiwi Matthew Sinclair had amassed 214 on his Test debut against the West Indies two years ago and arrived in Sharjah with 917 runs (av. 51.21) from only 13 Tests. Selectors had used him sparingly in one-dayers, fearing the shortened form of the game might harm his technique. This was talented Sinclair's first Sharjah tour and he didn't disappoint, scoring 304 runs in four matches, including two centuries. Sinclair wanted to use Sharjah as a guide to how well he would handle the champion subcontinent spinners on their home grounds. (Sinclair, yet to tour Sri Lanka, India or Pakistan, certainly got his answer, finishing the tournament with an average of 102.)

Sinclair provided the individual brilliance, but Pakistan were teamwork personified and the side's all-round ability was much in evidence in the pool matches. Sri Lanka didn't fire on all cylinders and even risked their spot in the final when New Zealand got up in the last preliminary game.

A sell-out, pro-Pakistan crowd watched the final, but found little to cheer. The oldest adage in cricket is, 'catches win matches' and the Pakistanis put down a number of chances at vital stages of the game. The experienced Sri Lankans rose to the occasion. Poor form of the past two weeks counted for nothing as they amassed a huge seven for 297, powered by fine innings from skipper Sanath Jayasuriya (70), Marvan Atapattu (89) and Mahela Jayawardene (67).

Pakistan started well, capturing an early wicket when Jayasuriya pushed Waqar to short mid on, started to run, then hesitated. Kaluwitharana, his opening partner, responded to the call, but couldn't make it back, despite Shoaib Malik's throw being off target and Waqar juggling the ball. Thereafter, it all went Sri Lanka's way.

Pakistan's bowling made little impression on Jayasuriya and Atapattu who piled on the runs, both appearing totally at ease. The first six of the match came from a Jayasuriya flourish over cover from the bowling of Waqar. Jayasuriya also hit Abdur Razzaq for two successive sixes. The big hits were shades of Jayasuriya's blitz against New Zealand in a pool match when he hit Chris Harris for a world record-equalling 30 off an over on his way to 107.

The skipper went for a number of risky shots in the final as he tried to speed the run rate in the final. On 44, he lofted Mohammed Sami to long-on, but the rival captain, Waqar Younis, dropped the catch. Jayasuriya was missed again, at 48, by wicketkeeper Humayun Farhat. However, the opener played some blistering shots, particularly square of the wicket. Jayasuriya eventually fell for 70, induced by Shoaib Malik to play a top-edge sweep to the safe hands of Inzamam at leg slip. Malik could have had Jayawardene next ball, but substitute Yasir Arafat put down a 'sitter' at deep square-leg.

The steady Atapattu brought up his 50 (which contained only two boundaries in 88 balls) and was promptly given a life when Inzamam failed to hold a sharp chance in the covers from Afridi's spin bowling.

Sri Lanka were two for 149 after 35 overs and it was time to put the foot down even further. Anchor-man Atapattu took some liberties and hit Malik for a big six. And another catch went down, Saqlain at deep square leg dropping Jayawardene on 35.

A fuming Waqar came back into the attack and bowled Atapattu with a fierce yorker, but it was signalled no ball. That seemed to sum up Pakistan's day.

Atapattu ran himself out, but not until he had scored 89. Jayawardene made 67, eventually caught and bowled Saqlain.

The Sri Lankans needed to conquer Waqar Younis, who was relishing the captaincy and had struck a rich vein of form in the pool matches. Two years after being 12th man for the World Cup final, he was Pakistan's main man. Jayawardene hit Waqar for two sixes in a row over mid wicket in the 47th over.

Pakistan, called upon to chase a run-rate of six per over, began disastrously. Imran Nazir was dropped off the first ball of the innings by Kaluwitharana off the bowling of Vaas. Imran put only five runs next to his name before Kaluwitharana held the next catch, this time off Nuwan Zoysa.

Thunderous applause greeted the arrival of Saeed Anwar to the crease, and he didn't disappoint his supporters. Of the frontline batsmen, Anwar (62) and Farhat (32) were the only Pakistani players to settle against either the onslaught of the Sri Lankan fast bowlers or the guile of the spinners. The pair put on 69 runs in 52 balls when a superb catch by Muralitharan at deep point from a Vaas lifter ended Farhat's innings.

Inzamam came in at number five. With only three runs to his name and the score on 95, he pulled Vaas hard, a shot that looked certain to go for four. Arnold leapt high at mid-wicket and held a scorching catch. Prospects of a Pakistani win were dim. Half the side were back in the pavilion by the 14th over. Younis Khan (4) soon fell to Vaas as he tried to drive without getting behind the line and was well caught by Jayawardene. The tail wagged through Malik (44) and Younis (20), but the result was beyond doubt.

Vaas (three for 36) and Zoysa (two for 51) were the most destructive of the Sri Lankan bowlers. Sri Lanka's fielding was as good as Pakistan's had been inept.

Such was the excitement that greeted Sri Lanka's team back in Colombo after winning the tri-nations tournament that armed guards promptly relieved Jayasuriya of the gold trophy, just to be certain it wasn't damaged or stolen.

Jayasuriya and his men arrived to a heroes' welcome and a message from President Chandrika Kumaratunga congratulating them on their success.

The one-kilo gold trophy, which the team won with the 77-run victory over Pakistan, along with $50,000 prize money, was immediately given an armed escort by guards who took it to a bank vault for safekeeping. The gold was worth about $9,000 at current market prices, officials said, adding that it was the first time that armed guards had been deployed to protect a trophy.

Even when Sri Lanka won the World Cup in March 1996 by beating Australia, the most prestigious prize in international cricket was not given such close protection.

Shahid Afridi prepares for battle

CHAPTER 35

PAKISTAN'S QUALITY HARD TO DISMISS

Pakistan arrived for Sharjah's 30th official international tournament in 20 years having left their country hovering on the fringe of the war in Afghanistan.

Post-September 11, 2001 uncertainty caused New Zealand to cancel a scheduled tour of Pakistan and the break left the subcontinent team underdone for Sharjah's last competition of that year.

Rumours abounded that the Sharjah tournament would also be cancelled, but the organisers would not hear of it. The CBFS also announced the appointment of a high-profile 'Ethics Committee' to scrutinise tournaments in Sharjah and banish match-fixing allegations forever. The three-man committee of impeccable pedigree comprised Clive Lloyd, Ian Botham and Sunil Gavaskar.

Joining Pakistan in the Khaleej Times Trophy series were Sri Lanka, the favourites for the event, and Zimbabwe, desperately hoping to arrest a string of losses.

Pakistan, again skippered by Waqar Younis, and Sri Lanka, with Sanath Jayasuriya again at the helm, boasted some newcomers, but essentially the core was the seasoned professionals. Hard-fought matches were guaranteed. Pakistan, however, continued to play musical chairs with the coaching role and this time it was Mudassar Nazar, the dignified former opening batsmanwho was in charge.

The facts concerning Zimbabwe were hardly ambiguous. Although the team rarely contained greats of the world stage, they often embarrassed the best of sides at Test or ODI level. Zimbabwe arrived in the Gulf with confidence at an all-time low having been beaten 5-0 by England and South Africa 3-0.

Brian Murphy, 24, a 'player of the future', as they say, was appointed captain of Zimbabwe when trusty campaigner Heath Streak said he couldn't take the strain anymore. Murphy, who made his Test debut against the West Indies at Port of Spain in 1999-2000, became captain after only 10 Tests and 17 ODIs.

"Obviously we have a lot of picking up to do," Murphy said upon arrival in Sharjah. "The guys were disappointed at those recent results, but that's history and we're working hard to reverse the trend."

Perhaps of greater significance than Murphy's appointment was Zimbabwe's recruitment of Geoff Marsh, the former opening batsman, as coach. The West Australian wheat farmer nicknamed 'Swampy' is held in the highest regard throughout the cricket world as a player, leader and motivator.

Pakistan's preparation for the tournament was far from ideal. The spectre of match fixing continued to haunt Pakistani cricket with a domestic

Heath Streak stood down as skipper

inquiry in full swing as the national side flew out. Younis, however, was determined not to be distracted in his bid to capture his first title as skipper.

"We haven't played international cricket for a while, but that also makes the players hungry for success," Younis said. "The cancellation of the New Zealand series gave the players the chance to fall back on domestic cricket and sort out problems. Lack of international cricket has kept the fire burning in

Brian Murphy took over as captain of Zimbabwe

the boys. I'm taking the tournament as a personal challenge because I haven't won a title as captain. It would be the icing on the cake if it came in Sharjah where we lost to Sri Lanka last time."

Sri Lanka arrived in the right frame of mind for victory. Organised, fearless and intelligent, they were aiming to complete a hat-trick of victories in the UAE. Pakistan and Zimbabwe would have to face the most rigorous examination of their respective strengths and weaknesses.

"Every day is a new day, but we do hope to continue in the same vein," said Jayasuriya, such a stylish and effective player whom both teams would need to limit to win the series.

The first match was between Zimbabwe and Sri Lanka and Marsh said of his new-found charges: "Zimbabwe are a team that always shows a lot of fighting qualities. They nibble away at the opposition."

But Sri Lanka barely moved out of second gear in inflicting a 63-run defeat on Zimbabwe, the 12th successive loss for the Africans. Sri Lanka posed the hard questions and Zimbabwe didn't have the answers. Old hands Atapattu (92) and Arnold (76) laid the groundwork with the bat, but the gamebreaker was debutant seamer Charitha Buddika who returned a haul of five for 67. Whatmore declares the young man is much more than "promising".

The losses kept coming for Zimbabwe, the worst a massive 106-run defeat at the hands of Pakistan. The tournament quickly became a two-horse race.

Pakistan and Sri Lanka made it to the final with three wins from four matches, both teams inflicting one defeat on each other.

Sri Lanka beat Pakistan by seven wickets in a match that exposed the lack of recent top-class cricket by Younis' team. Pakistan were all out for 178 with the top order capitulating to Dilhara Fernando (7-0-43-3), a bowler whose streamlined action allows plenty of variation. Gunawardene's innings of 88 helped make short work of the chase.

Younis conceded his men were "a bit rusty", but added, "it's no excuse."

Inzamam ul-Haq on the attack

Waqar Younis receives the Khaleej Times Trophy

A quietly satisfied Jayasuriya said: "Things are moving according to plan"

However, Pakistan struck a major psychological blow in the final pool match. Emerging opener Naveed Latif (113) and modern-day great Inzamam ul-Haq (118) put Sri Lanka to the sword. Latif was a bit of a mystery outside Pakistan, but those good old judges who take notes on the boundary in places like Quetta, Lahore, Karachi and Multan, regard him as his country's next top-tier batsman.

Pakistan's top-order batsmen often bat with flourish when the bottom order looks full of runs. They seem to like that extra confidence.

As for Inzamam, he has a very short backlift and is gutsy and straight-forward in approach. He's never intimidated. This was a typical innings by the big man as he pulled, cut and drove with great power.

The centurions showed scant respect for the attack which looked lame without the champion spinner Muttiah Muralitharan who was absent due to a sore shoulder. The other bowlers were made to look mere trundlers. Sri Lanka's total of nine for 272 in 50 overs was overhauled in 49.2 overs for the loss of only three wickets.

The match, worthy of the final, will also be remembered for Jayasuriya's passing of the personal milestone of 7,000 runs in ODI cricket. With a regulation single from a Shahid Afridi delivery, Jayasuriya, who scored 36 in this match, reached the 7,000 mark. He became only the third Sri Lankan batsman after Aravinda de Silva (8,430) and Arjuna Ranatunga (7,456) to do so.

Younis and Jayasuriya tossed the coin for the final, the 181st match at Sharjah and the 63rd in the emirate under floodlights. It was also the 28th game between Pakistan and Sri Lanka. Pakistan had won

16, Sri Lanka 10 and one ended in a tie.

The final failed to reach great heights. Pakistan blasted out Sri Lanka for 173 with Akram (8-0-20-2) and Younis (8.2-1-31-3) in devastating form. This Sri Lankan batting line-up was much stronger than it appeared on paper as an historic Test series victory over the West Indies in a few months time was to prove, but here in Sharjah most batsmen lost their wickets flashing at balls they should have left alone.

Pakistan made the perfect start when Younis had Gunawardene, who played some brilliant strokes on both sides of the wicket throughout this tournament, caught in slips by Azhar Mahmood for two.

Most sides feel more comfortable when Atapattu is tucked away in the pavilion and Akram obliged. The first-drop fenced at a ball from the veteran left-arm quick that would have been called wide if he hadn't gone after it. The dismissal gave 'keeper Rashid Latif the first of his four catches, all brought about by poor judgment outside the off stump rather than incisive bowling.

Opener Jayasuriya remained at the crease. The Sri Lankan captain scored 34 off 58 balls, including five fours, and appeared comfortable in the anchor role. Jayasuriya and Mahela Jayardene put on 58 for the third wicket and seemed to be steering Sri Lanka into the comfort zone. The pro-Pakistani crowd of 22,000 went up as one when spinner Afridi tempted Jayasuriya outside off stump. The rash shot attracted a thick edge which was gleefully accepted by Latif.

Russell Arnold went about the task in his typically cavalier manner. He middled the ball early and looked impregnable. Arnold came up with some of the best shots of the tournament and he and Jayawardene also annoyed Pakistan with quick singles.

Jayardene's promising innings came to an end at 43 off 51 balls, with four fours, when Latif held a catch from Akhtar's bowling, a ball that looked particularly fast.

Arnold continued to attack and closed on a half century. A big score was likely until he was hit on the pad by Akram. The ball seemed to be going down leg side, but South African umpire Rudy Koertzen held the opposite opinion. A stunned and dejected Arnold stood his ground and repeatedly shook his head in disbelief.

Pakistan's bowling was too good to permit the tide to turn against them. After 44.2 overs they showered and prepared to defend a small target on a good batting strip.

Afridi (35) and Naveed Latif (23) gave Pakistan a good start, but they failed to consolidate. Yousuf Youhana (40) and the cool Inzamam (28) steered Pakistan towards victory although they weren't at the crease in the end. Pakistan lost five wickets in scoring 177 in 43.4 overs.

Sri Lanka's only hope, a slender one at that, was the record-breaking spinner Muralitharan, the gentle young man with the twisted elbow. As it was, the game-breaking bowler picked up the wickets of Afridi, Naveed Latif and Inzamam, but it was too little, too late for Sri Lanka.

Granted, Pakistan were patchy in the pool matches. They needed a slice of luck mixed with a handful of their typical grit to take the trophy, but victory was well deserved.

Younis paid tribute to Akram's bowlng: "Wasim has been providing us with the vital breakthroughs throughout the tournament and they made a big difference."

The skipper said there were not any anxious moments during the final, but acknowledged that small targets have the potential to cause attacks of the jitters.

"Smaller targets can lead to batsmen getting careless. In chasing the big ones you have a broader frame of mind."

Jayasuriya felt the loss in the pool match wounded his team psychologically and the players didn't recover.

"In the final we needed to make 230-240 to make a match of it. Unfortunately, we couldn't."

Younis' rousing performance with the ball earned him man-of-the-match honours. The consistency of Jayawardene won him man-of-the-series.

However, no sooner had the applause died down for Pakistan's Sharjah triumph then the chucking chorus was heard again concerning Akhtar's controversial action.

Akhtar was reported for a suspect action for the second time during the year (and third time in all) in the Sharjah final. The 26-year-old dubbed the 'Rawalpindi Express' saw his career put in doubt. The International Cricket Council (ICC) responded by appointing former West Indian fast bowler Michael Holding to work with Akhtar on his action. Under ICC rules a player can face a 12-month ban if reported for throwing three times in a year.

The protracted controversy concerning one of the world's fastest and most exciting young bowlers soon took another twist when the Pakistan Cricket Board (PCB) announced Akhtar had been cleared for a second time by Australian experts. PCD director Brigadier Munawwar Rana said in Karachi that he had received a new report on the fast bowler from the University of Western Australia.

"The report confirms and reiterates its earlier findings of May 2001 that it is Shoaib's peculiar anatomical characteristics that led to the erroneous perception of throwing. The university has reaffirmed that Shoaib has had an abnormal upper limb in his bowling arm since birth," said Rana. The PCB asked the ICC to study medical reports and consider Aktar's action as a special case.

Biomechanics experts in Perth, Western Australia, where Akhtar was sent, had argued that video analysis showed his action was legal. They said it looked as if his arm was straightening during delivery because of the abnormal flexibility of his shoulder and elbow joints. Rana said they confirmed their findings after studying a video of Akhtar's bowling action during the last Sharjah tournament.

Akhtar, who had barely played over the past year because of a shoulder injury, had a long chat with the author in Sharjah, mainly about the frustrations of being sidelined and how the wear-and-tear forced him to alter his approach and attitude to bowling.

"The injury is coming along, but I'm being really careful with it," he said. "I'm trying to make better use of the ball, use the conditions to a greater degree, let the ball do the work. The pace is coming back, but I'm building up to the faster balls and I'm definitely not trying to bowl flat out every ball. I'm concentrating more on thinking while I'm bowling and making more use of things like the reverse swing."

Shortly after the interview Akhtar collected his bags at Sydney's Kingsford Smith Airport and was driven over the famous Harbour Bridge. The express bowler signed for a short stint of cricket with the Mosman Club in Sydney's weekend grade competition. Mosman is a quiet, leafy suburb in one of the more well-heeled parts of the city. The cricket team is always fiercely competitive and Allan Border first played for Australia out of Mosman.

Akhtar joined his friend Brett Lee, his leading rival for world's fastest bowler, in the Mosman XI. A joke

Geoff Marsh (left) chats with Shoaib Akhtar in the players' enclosure at Sharjah

(not funny if you were padding up) went around town as fast as a Lee Yorker or Akhtar bouncer, that Sydney's opening batsmen all prayed their captains won the toss against Mosman – and promptly elected to field.

The rumble of the bombing raids over Afghanistan grew stronger. Pakistan's border hospitals created ubiquitous and frightening 'war wards'. Pakistan became pivotal in a deadly international chess game. Then Kabul, the capital of Afghanistan, fell. Siege was laid on Kandahar in southern Afghanistan. Refugees jammed the barbed wire outpost at Chamam, a little frontier town on the Pakistan-Afghanistan border. Pakistan, which already had three million refugees from Afghanistan, prepared for many more.

For Waqar Younis, Wasim Akram and Saeed Anwar there was not much celebration of the Sharjah success. Anwar has become even more dedicated to his Islamic faith following the death of his three-year-old daughter. The three cricketers called a press conference in Lahore, nothing to do with cricket, to lend their support to the Afghan refugees. You can let some causes pass through to the 'keeper, but others are far beyond the game and must be played straight and true … Inshallah.

CHAPTER 36

HAPPY BIRTHDAY

Pakistan gave Sharjah the most appropriate 21st birthday present in the 2002 Sharjah Cup - wholesale slaughter of Sri Lanka in a final. Pakistan also set course for the World Cup.

It was the 191st one-day international at Sharjah Stadium as well as Pakistan's 104th and Sri Lanka's 72nd match at the ground. But the statistic that really counted was that the Lankans were beaten by the staggering margin of 217 runs. It took Pakistan a mere 16.5 overs to reduce a hitherto in-form opposition to nine for 78. Muttiah Muralitharan couldn't bat due to a shoulder injury and at least he was lucky to be in hospital during the capitulation.

Waqar Younis, the Pakistan captain, said at the outset of this three-pronged tournament - the third side was New Zealand - that his team was starting the build-up to the 2003 World Cup. The Sri Lankans, who found passage to the final easier than Pakistan, would have been wise to take note of the fast bowler's comments when he arrived in the UAE.

"Although there is a lot of cricket to be played before next year's World Cup I hope we can win this tri-series to open our campaign," he said.

A pensive Imran Nazir waits his turn

Pakistan were at their merciless best in the final. They have a habit of reserving Sharjah for grand deeds and this was no exception.

Pakistan batted first and Imran Nazir, back in the team after a year's absence, repaid the selectors' faith with 63. Nazir likes the Sharjah ground and it seems to like him. He scored his second half-century of this tournament and passed 1,000 runs in international one-day cricket. Fellow opener Afridi (14) and first-drop Latif (0) went quickly, clean bowled by Zoysa and Vaas respectively, but it didn't do Sri Lanka any favours as it brought Yousuf Youhana to the wicket earlier.

This was Youhana's day. Out of sorts in recent times, he played a grand innings of 129, as good as some of the best from Tendulkar and Lara. Yousuf is probably better known for his Test batting but this knock - 131 balls, eight fours, three sixes - was the equal of anything he has played in the five-day form of the game. It was also his highest score in limited overs internationals and, appropriately, he did it in his 100th one-dayer.

Younis Khan kept the scoreboard ticking over, but was content to let his partner's bat do most of the talking. Younis scored 66, but of greater importance was the huge 155-run stand he put on with Youhana for the fifth wicket. It only ended with two balls of the regulation 50 overs left when Younis holed out on the leg side, caught Atapattu bowled Zoysa. Youhana was out next ball, also attempting a long hit off Zoysa and being caught by Buddhika. Their efforts were needed too because Inzamam ul-Haq had earlier turned the clock back and ran himself out for 12.

Sri Lanka's hopes of stemming the furious tide were dented when Muralitharan slipped making a routine stop and fell on his left shoulder. The brilliant bowler was immediately helped off, in considerable pain, by the team physio. Ligament damage was diagnosed and the record-breaking off-spinner was flown to Australia for assessment by medical specialists. A period of rest was prescribed, but he avoided surgery.

Pakistan took advantage of Muralitharan's absence from the attack, posting 295 for the loss of six wickets.

The asking rate nudged six an over when Sanath Jayasuriya and Marvan Atapattu went out to confront the Pakistani speedsters. The had to take risks, bat well and enjoy a few hefty slices of luck. Waqar, Akram, Akhtar and Saqlain Mushtaq, whose return to form improved the balance of the attack, were the main obstacles.

Akram is probably the world's best at breaking opening partnerships early in the piece. Atapattu jammed the bat down on an Akram yorker only to see the ball spin back on to his wicket.

Jayasuriya went for his shots and hit up 19. Younis brought Akhtar into the attack and he was quick to respond to his captain's call for a wicket. Akhtar dropped one in short and the living legend of Sri Lankan cricket miscued a pull to give the overjoyed fast bowler a valuable caught and bowled.

Akram struck again next over, trapping pinch-hitter Vaas dead in front. From there it was basically a wicket per over with Akhtar's figures a deadly three for 11. Akram recorded two for 33 and Younis who destroyed the tail, finished with three for 33.

Sri Lanka were expected to perform best in the final as they were first team through and had three wins out of four games. Pakistan and New Zealand, who had a win apiece, were forced to battle it out for the other spot.

Sri Lanka set the Black Caps 244 for victory and only permitted nine for 197 in reply.

The Kiwis had a poor tournament, but they did pull off a miraculous victory over Sri Lanka. Defending a paltry total of 218 New Zealand overcame a devastating spell by Muralitharan to stun Sri Lanka with an 11-run victory.

The versatile off-spinner produced an extraordinary 10-over spell in which he grabbed five wickets for nine runs as New Zealand were restricted to 218-8. But the Kiwis fought back in the field to bowl out Sri Lanka for 207 in 49.1 overs despite a horrific butter-fingered display by wicketkeeper Chris Nevin, who stepped in to the team following the retirement of Adam Parore. Nevin dropped Atapattu thrice and missed a run out, but Daryl Tuffy took three catches and Scott Styris claimed three wickets to fashion a remarkable win. Atapattu rode on Nevin's generosity to make 61, but found no support at the other end as the last five wickets crashed for 34 runs.

New Zealand won despite injuries to four key bowlers, including star all-rounder Chris Cairns and paceman Shane Bond.

It was a pity that Nathan Astle, whose cavalier batting lit up his country's Tests against Australia and England throughout the 2001-02 season, was out of sorts throughout the Sharjah tournament. He flew to the UAE having been named New Zealand Player of

the Year and excitement was expected every time he strode to the crease. This was because the Canterbury batsman scored the fastest Test 200 ever from just 153 balls against England in Christchurch. He finished the three-Test series with a batting average of 62.80.

New Zealand, in Sharjah following a wonderful Test and one-day series in Australia and some heroics against England as well, headed to Pakistan for their rescheduled one-day and Test rubber. The series had to be postponed in the terrible aftermath of September 11, 2001.

In the final of the Sharjah Cup, 21 years since the Gavaskar-Miandad XI brought the sport to the UAE at international level, Yousuf Youhana - a mere toddler when that game took place - won man-of-the-match honours. Marvan Atapattu's consistency garnered him man-of-the-series and Muthiah Muralitharan was officially the tournament's top bowler.

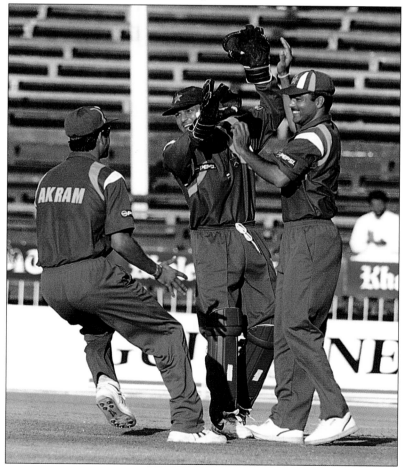

The Pakistanis have had plenty to celebrate at Sharjah over the years

CHAPTER 37

TEST TIME

Australia v England 1876-77
The Melbourne Cricket Ground, Melbourne
March 15, 16, 17, 18 1877
Australia won by 45 runs
Australia 245 (C. Bannerman 165 retired hurt) and
104: England 196 (H. Jupp 63, W.E. Midwinter five
for 78) and 108 (T.Kendall seven for 55)

This was the first official Test match.

England was represented by professional players who had been touring Australia during the 1876-77 season, but it would have been a stronger team had it included the leading amateur players of the day.

Australia won the toss and batted first. Charles Bannerman dominated the innings and, after receiving the first ball in Test cricket, went on to score the first century. He eventually retired hurt after making 165 in an Australian total of 245. Surrey opener Harry Jupp top-scored in England's first innings with a patient knock of 63. A collection at the ground raised 165 pounds. (The idea of benefits for cricketers isn't quite so new…)

Pakistan versus West Indies
Sharjah Cricket Association Stadium, Sharjah,
United Arab Emirates
January 31, February 1,2,3,4 2002
Pakistan won by 170 runs
Pakistan 493 (Yousuf Youhana 146, Rashid Latif 150) and 214 (M. Dillon three for 18).
  West Indies 264 (D. Ganga 65, C.L Hooper not out 84; Shoaib Akhtar four for 63) and 366 (CH Gayle 68, W.W Hinds 59, CL Hooper 56, S. Chanderpaul 66, R.O Hinds 62; Waqar Younis four for 93)

This was the world's first bilateral Test match on neutral ground in the 126-year history of the game. It was contested between two of the game's great powers, Pakistan and West Indies. The Sharjah series was a 'home' rubber for Pakistan. The West Indies feared for player safety because of military action in neighbouring Afghanistan and tension between India and Pakistan over the disputed region of Kashmir.

The Pakistan Cricket Board said the decision to play the series in Sharjah was taken "in the best interest of the game and the players."

Brig. Munawar Ahmed Rana, director of the PCB, said: "We still do hold out that Pakistan is safe for cricket. The Sri Lankan Under-19 team has been here, Clive Lloyd found it safe enough during a coaching assignment, the English team is happy to be in the subcontinent (England played three Tests and six one-dayers December 2001-January 2002 although several leading players declined to tour). However we do not wish to involve the ICC in this, aggravating the matter and causing further trouble for them. We will go ahead and play at a third venue. Financially, the tour may find it difficult to break even. We will certainly evaluate the matter of financial losses."

The PCB said it lost $25 million in 2001 because of cancelled visits by India, New Zealand and Sri Lanka.

The PCB statement was issued months before a suicide bombing in Karachi outside the Sheraton Hotel when 11 people were killed. New Zealand had eventually toured Pakistan and the touring team was staying relatively close to where the bomb went off. Some officials of the Karachi Test were in the Sheraton when the explosion happened. Some Kiwi players encountered survivors of the blast with limbs missing. The tour was aborted and the Black Caps flew home. Players were offered trauma counselling.

Originally scheduled to play three Tests, three one-day matches and warm-up matches over six weeks in Pakistan, the West Indies contested two Tests and three one-dayers in Sharjah. There were no official practice matches.

The international political backdrop may have been far from ideal, but 21 years after a cricket-loving Arab put up some scaffolding and fashioned a one-day game between some top-level players, Test cricket came to his precious green field in Sharjah.

Controversy built up before the historic first 'offshore Test' and it had nothing do with the venue being switched from Pakistan due to the distant thunder of the bombing raids over Afghanistan or the huge anti-US protests on the streets of most Pakistani cities.

Two months after sparking a dispute in South Africa that threatened to split cricket, Mike Denness returned as a referee, to Sharjah. Pakistan and West Indies welcomed his appointment. It was Denness' first job as referee since he disciplined six Indians in the second Test against South Africa.

"There was no deliberation when we agreed to Mike standing," said West Indies Cricket Board chief executive Gregory Shillingford. "He was referee for our series with South Africa (in 2001) and he had an excellent series."

Following Denness' action in the Port Elizabeth Test in November, 2001, India threatened to boycott the third match if he officiated. The ruling body backed the referee, who was then fired by the two nations. The match was then stripped of official Test status and a four-day standoff ensued between the International Cricket Council and the Indian Board.

"We have no problem with Denness," said Brigadier Rana. "The matter was between India and South Africa."

Down to the cricket...

Pakistan, an integral part of Sharjah's limited-overs tournament since 1984, would not only feel at home, but also have the luxury of a Test wicket prepared by Lahore-based groundsman Mohammed Bashir.

"I'm disappointed the series had to be shifted, but this place is like a second home to us," said Pakistan's skipper Waqar Younis. There was additional affinity for him as he had spent his early years in the Gulf emirate and his earliest memories of international cricket were autograph hunting at the ground where he would lead his country.

West Indies faced a formidable challenge in the absence of their batting genius Brian Lara. The left-hander, who had just countered the great Muralitharan with an amazing aggregate of 688 runs in three Tests in Sri Lanka, dislocated his left elbow in a freak collision with fielder Marvan Atapattu in a subsequent one-dayer.

To make matters worse, promising middle-order batsman Ramnaresh Sarwan was ruled out of the Sharjah series due to injury. The 21-year-old was the next best batsman after Lara in Sri Lanka, making 318 runs in that series. Luckily, the seasoned duo of Shivnarine Chanderpaul and Sherwin Campbell were back to lend experience to the line-up after battling injury and poor form.

"It's good to have them back," said Carl Hooper, the captain and 90-Test veteran. "We are grooming young players and this process will take time. At the moment we're just happy to be playing Test cricket, whether it is in Pakistan or in Sharjah..."

The first Test in Sharjah was the 38th between the two nations. The West Indies had won 19, Pakistan 18 and there had been 14 draws. Pakistan's highest Test score against the West Indies remains 657 at Kingston

West Indies skipper Carl Hooper bowling at Sharjah Stadium during the historic Test series

during the 1957-58 series while the West Indies' highest is 790 in the same game. Sir Garfield Sobers holds the record for highest individual score between the two countries and for the West Indies against Pakistan with his 365 not out, also in this game at Kingston. Hanif Mohammed scored 337 at Bridgetown in the 1957 series, the highest individual total by a Pakistani against the West Indies.

THE FIRST TEST

And so it came to pass… Pakistan won the toss and batted in the first Test at Sharjah.

Pakistan were wary and only three boundaries came from the first 29 overs. There was none of the one-day tournament jousting as Pakistan, who struggled to reach two for 45 by lunch against the disciplined West Indians, slipped to four for 94 before recovering to post five for 230 by stumps.

Debutant opener Naved Latif, surprisingly included ahead of Shahid Afridi, found a special place in cricket history when he became the first player dismissed in a Test at Sharjah. He was trapped lbw by Mervyn Dillon in the third over after facing six deliveries.

His opening partner, Taufiq Umer, scored 24 before edging a ball from off-spinner and captain Carl Hooper on to his stumps. Surprisingly, Hooper left out the team's only specialist spinner, Dinanath

Campbell just makes it home as Rashid Latif breakes the stumps at Sharjah Stadium

Ramnarine, to play three fast bowlers. The West Indies gave a Test cap to left-handed all-rounder Ryan Hinds of Barbados who had the additional responsibility of sharing the spin duties with Hooper.

Yousuf Youhana, who made 204 not out in his last Test innings earlier in the month against Bangladesh, kept up the fine form to be unconquered on 78 at stumps.

Younis Khan and Inzamam ul-Haq took Pakistan to two for 80 after lunch when both fell in the space of five overs playing rash shots outside the off stump. Inzamam, one of the game's most explosive Test batsmen, made 10 in 40 minutes before he slashed in frustration against Dillon and was easily caught by wicketkeeper Ridley Jacobs.

Younis Khan contributed 53 to the scoreboard, but cut Hooper into the hands of Chris Gayle at slip. It was the fifth-wicket stand of 84 between Youhana and Abdur Razzaq that held back the spirited West Indian challenge led by two wickets apiece from Hooper and Dillon. However, it was part-timer Wavell Hinds who earned the crucial breakthrough in the final session when he had Razzaq edge a catch to Jacobs after he scored 34. Rashid Latif was not out 27 at stumps having added 52 valuable runs for the sixth wicket with Youhana.

The West Indies were to rue a missed catch off Youhana when Cameron Cuffy put down a low chance at mid-on off Dillon's bowling. Two balls later Youhana responded with a six over square leg.

The day saw tough, uncomplicated, no-frills cricket. In other words, a typical first day of a Test match.

The next day belonged to Youhana and Latif who both scored centuries as Pakistan tightened their grip. The pair shared in a sixth-wicket stand of 204 before Pakistan were bowled out for 493 midway through the final session, Latif, who had a number of lives, top-scoring with a career-best 150 and Youhana making 146.

Youhana, who came into this match with over 2,500 Test runs at an average of 47 in 57 innings, signalled his intentions with a cracking straight-drive to the boundary as his first scoring shot of the morning.

Playing in his 36th Test, Youhana reached three figures for the ninth time at Test level, and his third against the West Indies in just four matches when he steered Pedro Collins to third man for a single. His century came in 264 minutes off 209 balls and contained 12 fours and a six. Latif reached his maiden

Test century after taking two runs off Ryan Hinds. He faced 165 balls in all with 14 fours and one six.

Youhana was finally dismissed in the afternoon session, clean bowled by paceman Cameron Cuffy after a marathon innings lasting just over six hours. In 276 balls, he struck 18 fours and a six.

Latif, dropped on 27 by slip Chris Gayle and on 133 by long-on Sherwin Campbell, then added 56 for the seventh wicket before Saqlain Mushtaq was caught and bowled off Dillon.

Gayle eventually bowled Latif, who completed 1,000 runs in Test cricket when he reached 98, for 150. In all, he batted for five and a half hours, faced 234 balls and hit 16 fours and two sixes, both from Hooper's

Yousuf Youhana had a sensational Sharjah Test series

bowing.

The innings was hard work for the West Indies bowlers and this was reflected in the best figures being the three for 140 returned by Dillon. The stout-hearted 27-year-old sent down 42 overs on the lifeless, unforgiving wicket.

The first mountain for the West Indies to climb on day three was to score 293 to avoid the follow on. They did it as the light faded over Sharjah, but five wickets were lost along the way. Three of the top five West Indies batsmen, Chris Gayle (68), Wavell Hinds (59) and Carl Hooper (56) scored attractive half-centuries, but did 't go on to make big scores. Ryan Hinds, batting at seven, kept his head down for an unbeaten 53, an impressive debut by any standards.

This crop of West Indian players didn't handle spin as well as they should which meant they would have a lot of trouble with Saqlain Mustaq. Dour Darren Ganga faced 94 balls for 20 without hitting a boundary when Saqlain trapped him in front. Chris Gayle used his feet and got to the pitch of the ball, defended well and picked the right balls to hit. Having crossed the boundary 13 times in his 68 off 117 balls, Gayle was bowled by a Saqlain top-spinner.

Sherwin Campbell was unlucky to be out for six, but his batting was so at sea it is unlikely he would have been around long anyway. Saqlain and fellow spinner Danish Kaneira tied him in knots. Umpire George Sharp gave Campbell out lbw shouldering arms to a Kaneria googly although the ball looked like it would clear the stumps.

Wavell Hinds used his feet to the spinners and looked better and better the longer he was at the crease, especially when driving down the ground. However, he was beaten in flight stepping down to Kaneira just when he looked set for a century. Latif had the bails off in a flash to end Hinds' innings of 59 (83 balls, 10 fours, one six).

With the coming together of the Guyanese pair of Hooper and Shivnarine Chanderpaul, so did West Indies genuine hopes as they possessed experience and were the best players of spin in the West Indian side. They drove, they chipped over the infield, they worked the ball for singles. Hooper played some superb drives and Chanderpaul put the spinners off line with dexterous use of the sweep shot.

The atmosphere grew heavy just before tea and the Pakistani medium pacers tried to get the reverse swing going. Hooper slowed the pace of the game and

concentrated more on defence, but an in-dipper from Abdur Razzaq didn't get up as much as he expected and he was trapped plumb for (56 (103 balls, eight fours).

The occasion didn't faze 21-year-old Test first-timer Ryan Hinds. Chanderpaul took the strike whenever he could, but by stumps the newcomer had scored a composed half-century.

Resuming on five for 325, the West Indies moved to five for 362 before Younis took control. Younis took four wickets for nine runs in the space of 29 balls to bundle the West Indies out for 366 and give Pakistan a lead of 127.

The West Indies had gone into a slide early on the fourth day as Younis, wicketless the previous day, really bent his back. Chanderpaul added 11 to his overnight score of 45 before dragging one from Younis on to his stumps. Hinds top-edged a pull from a short ball that was on him before he knew it. Dillon was run out then Younis grabbed Cameron Cuffy and Ridley Jacobs to end the innings and return figures of 25.3-4-93-4.

Pakistan started poorly in their second innings. Naved Latif, who made a duck in the first innings, edged Dillon through to the 'keeper when he was 20. His opening partner Taufeeq Umar played some good drives through the off-side on his way to 23 when he was run out in a bad mix-up with Younis Khan.

The score was two for 54 and the situation a bit tricky, but Inzamam put things right with 48 (56 balls, five fours) before he became Dillon's second victim. Cuffy had Younis Khan (32), who hit a huge six off Hooper, caught behind, but a quick 47 not out by Rashid Latif (42 balls, four fours) enabled Pakistan to declare on seven for 214, leaving West Indies 342 for victory.

West Indian openers Darren Ganga (19) and Chris Gayle negotiated the fire and brimstone of the remaining 10 overs of the day, taking the West Indies to 24 for no loss. Hooper's men trailed by 317 and a thrilling final day was on the cards because the West Indies would certainly accept the challenge of the run chase.

The final day of the historic Test saw Shoaib Akhtar and Abdur Razzaq cause a sensational West Indian collapse and lead Pakistan to a resounding 170-run victory.

Akhtar picked up a career-best five for 24 and Razzaq took four for 25 as the West Indians lost nine wicket for 56 runs – the last seven for 25 – to be bundled out for 171 at tea. Ironically, the collapse followed a solid start which took the West Indies to one for 115 soon after lunch.

Akhtar put aside the controversy over his bowling action to work up terrifying pace to better his previous best of five for 43 against South Africa at Durban in 1998. He beat batsmen with raw speed and Razzaq was also fast. This is reflected in seven West Indian batsmen being either bowled or lbw.

Akhtar began the destruction in the third over after lunch when he clean bowled the dangerous Gayle who scored 66 with 15 boundaries. An Akhtar lifter next over was so fast it took the glove off Wavell Hinds and wicketkeeper Rashid Latif snaffled the catch. It was Latif's 100th dismissal in his 28th Test.

Tragedy struck when third umpire Athar Zaidi ruled Sherwin Campbell (20) run out as he attempted a quick single. Camera angles seemed to show Campbell made his ground.

Razzaq stepped up to remove Chanderpaul, Hooper and Jacobs in one over to reduce the West Indies to seven for 150. Chanderpaul was caught behind while Hooper and Jacobs were lbw in successive balls. Razzaq was denied a hat-trick, as was Akhtar who bowled Dillon and Cuffy off successive balls.

The last-wicket pair of Ryan Hinds and Collins put on 16 before Razzaq bowled Collins for 12 to put the West Indies out of their misery.

The world's first offshore Test was over... 21 years after the dream began.

THE SECOND TEST

As if times weren't difficult enough for the West Indies, they went into the second Test without batsmen Marlon Samuels and Sherwin Campbell who both sustained injuries.

A magnetic resonance imaging scan revealed that a problem with the inner part of Samuels' knee had developed over time following arthroscopic knee surgery that the player had had two years ago. A Dubai surgeon performed corrective surgery but Samuels was out of cricket seven weeks. Campbell, the former West Indies vice-captain, had his return to international cricket short-circuited by a broken little finger on his right hand.

The West Indies were down before the Test and definitely out at the end of it. Pakistani captain Waqar

Younis, enjoying a new lease on life, grabbed four for 44 on his way to joining the elite 350-wicket club as he led a 244-run rout of the West Indies. Playing his 78th Test, the fast bowler became only the third Pakistani after Wasim Akram (414) and Imran Khan (362) to reach the landmark.

"It's a big achievement for me, but I'm not finished yet," he said. "I look forward to going to 400 and more."

Pakistan, put in by Hooper, dominated West Indies on day one of the Test with Shahid Afridi (107) and Younis Khan (not out 131) having centuries up by stumps. Hooper's men had missed five chances and the Pakistanis made them pay. When Afridi was out Pakistan were sitting pretty at two for 202.

Khan kept up the good work next day and was finally dismissed caught by Ganga off Collins for 150.

Abdur Razzaq (not out 64) and Yousuf Youhana (60)

Mervyn Dillon bowled his heart out for the West Indies during the Test series

kept the pressure on and Pakistan were all out for a hefty 472.

Dinanath Ramnarine took three wickets for the West Indies, but they cost him 137 runs.

Ganga scored 65 before being bowled by Afridi then Hooper stood alone in trying to save a Test that had already slipped from grasp. Hooper farmed the strike and played some wonderful shots, in the process scoring his 5,000th Test run, only the ninth West Indian batsman to achieve this feat. Hooper ws unconquered on 84.

West Indies fell nine runs short of the target needed to avoid the follow-on. In the end it didn't matter because Younis didn't enforce it.

Enjoying a mammoth first innings lead of 208,

Rashid Latif plays another superb shot during the Test series

Pakistan made five for 225 in their second innings with the top scorers being Younis Khan (71), Taufeeq Umar (69) and Yousuf Youhana (not out 52). Dillon again tried his heart out and took three wickets for 57 in an 18-over spell.

To achieve victory the West Indies, without Brian Lara, needed to set a world record and catch the fourth innings target of 434. The highest a team has ever scored when batting last to win was four for 406 made by India against the West Indies at Port of Spain in 1976.

Set the improbable victory target of 434, the West Indies paid dearly for shoddy batting and two dubious umpiring decisions to be bundled out for a paltry 189 at the stroke of stumps on the fourth day.

Pakistan, buoyed by the 170-run victory in the first Test, were dismissive of West Indies' efforts. Either Younis blasted out the opposition in the second innings or all-rounder Abdur Razzaq (three for 33) picked up the important wickets.

Poor batting and inexperience by the top order and critical umpiring decisions diffused any slim hopes the West Indies may have entertained of pulling of a win.

Younis trapped Chris Gayle in front to take Test wicket number 349. The magical 350th should have come two overs later when Wavell Hinds edged an outswinger waist-high to Shahid Afridi at third slip, but the chance was grassed.

With the score on one for 46 Darren Ganga was adjudged out by Australian umpire Darrel Hair although TV replays showed Shoaib Akhtar's ball missing leg stump. An even greater tragedy followed one run later when Hooper, top-scorer for his side with an unbeaten 84 in the first innings, was given out lbw to Saqlain Mushtaq. Replays indicated the ball pitched outside off stump and turned only slightly, but Pakistani umpire Shakeel Khan raised his finger as soon as the bowler appealed.

Wavell Hinds tried his best, but was deceived by Saqlain's straight ball and edged a catch to substitute wicket-keeper Taufiq Umer, standing in for Rashid Latif who had injured his hand. Ryan Hinds hit 46 and Ridley Jacobs an unbeaten 35 to prolong the innings before Younis and Razzaq cleaned up the tail and sealed Pakistan's victory.

It was Pakistan's sixth Test win on the trot, and also the sixth time they scored well over 400 runs in the first innings of a match.

CHAPTER 38

WAQAR'S WINNING WAY

Pakistan maintained their winning streak in the one-day tournament that followed the historic Test series. However, in the third and final match Carl Hooper grafted on to his natural West Indian flair the fruits of wide experience and immaculate technique to score a superlative face-saving century.

Pakistan recovered from a dreadful start of three for 15 in game one to overhaul a poor West Indies total of 191 with four wickets and nearly four overs to spare.

Hooper won the toss and elected to bat on a dream pitch. Akram, on the comeback trail from injury, started with a wide then was sent to the point boundary next ball by Darren Ganga. Ganga did the same to Waqar Younis soon after but then stood on his stumps to give the Pakistan captain and his team their first wicket. Wavell Hinds also went cheaply, a victim of Shoaib Akhtar who came on first change.

Waqar Younis... another triumph

Gayle played a stroke-filled innings of 50 (52 balls, 10 fours) and was particularly savage on Akram, hitting him for three boundaries in one over. Gayle also took three boundaries from Abdur Razzaq and looked on course for a three-figure total but played a lazy shot to Razzaq and was bowled.

The West Indies were reasonably well placed at two for 95 after 18 overs, but by 25 overs were teetering at five for 117. Hooper and Jacobs tried to calm the middle order but Pakistan denied them scoring opportunities. While 16 fours were hit in the first 17 overs, the West Indies did not score any boundaries between overs 22 and 45.

A typically stylish shot by Shivnarine Chanderpaul

Hooper was trapped leg-before by Afridi on 45 (81 balls, three fours) in the 40th over and that put paid to West Indies chances of a reasonable total. Jacobs went for 25 after a clumsy attempt at a sweep. The tail crumbled.

Pakistan clinched the one-day series in spectacular fashion. Shoaib Malik scored a dazzling, unbeaten century and Mohammed Sami then applied the blow-torch with a hat-trick to power Pakistan to a 51-run victory, their ninth in a row, with more than 15 overs in hand.

Talk about grasping opportunities with both hands. The match-winning duo came into the side in place of regulars Saqlain Mushtaq and Wasim Akram who were rested.

There was also some experimentation with Inzamam ul-Haq being asked to open the innings in the hope he would recapture some form. It was not to be, and a clearly out-of-touch Inzamam flashed at a wide delivery from Cameron Cuffy and essentially

Shoaib Akhtar in full cry

guided it into the safe hands of Gayle at first slip to be dismissed for three.

Merv Dillon dropped a caught and bowled chance off Afridi in the first over, but he made amends when the 'Pathan Cowboy' offered him another chance. Dillon held this one and Afridi was out for four. Pakistan were two for seven, and struggling. Malik and Younis Khan tried to bat Pakistan out of trouble but Cuffy, whose four overs out of the first five were maidens and Dillon, also bowling a good line, waged a war of attrition.

Younis Khan (18) was lbw to Cuffy, trying to repeat a boundary to long-on the previous ball. Youhana (1) was also trapped in front, by Collymore.

Pakistan were in trouble at four for 51 in the 17th over before Malik launched into the West Indies attack. Malik brought up his 50 off 90 balls. He flicked big Dillon off his toes to long-leg to bring up the magical three figures. The 20-year-old all-rounder from Sialkot's unbeaten 111 was his first ton in 20 ODI matches. It came off 130 balls and included nine fours and a six.

It was generally a poor effort from the West Indies because Pakistan's total of 232 was definitely within reach.

Despite Ganga going for a duck, caught behind by Latif off Younis from the first ball of the innings, Gayle and Wavell Hinds put on 101 runs in 91 balls before Hinds was out for 29. Gayle's batting was daring and cavalier and he scored 62 off 45 deliveries including six fours and three sixes. Two of the sixes were off Akhtar and one off Younis.

The men in the red caps slipped from one for 101 to five for 133. Pakistan's captain got the big wicket of his counterpart Hooper (7) right in front. Sami got one through the gate to send the debutant Runako Morton on his way for 16.

Chanderpaul and Ryan Hinds batted steadily in a stand of 45 for the sixth wicket but Abdur Razzaq, back for his second spell, claimed both their wickets in one over. However, the real bowling fireworks were yet to come. Sami got Ridley Jacobs lbw then bowled Corey Collymore and Cameron Cuffy to go into the record books as one of the elite players to have taken hat-tricks at international level. Indeed, Sami became only the sixth Pakistani player to achieve the feat after Wasim Akram, Waqar Younis, Jalaluddin, Aaqib Javed and Saqlain Mushtaq.

* * *

Hooper played a superb captain's knock of 112 not out as the West Indies gained a consolation 110-run victory over Pakistan in the third and final game.

Hooper's seventh one-day century helped the West Indies pile up five for 260 before Pakistan were shot out for 150 in the 40.2 overs in this inconsequential match

It was the West Indies first success after four defeats in the desert world in three weeks. They had, of course, lost the two Test matches by heavy margins before being soundly beaten in the first two one-dayers.

Hooper smashed eight boundaries and four sixes, sharing a 154-run stand for the fifth wicket with Shivnarine Chanderpaul (67), after the West Indies were reduced to four for 61. It was a treat for Sharjah to see the true quality of Hooper's batting. He is a beautifully balanced batsman of impeccable poise and timing. This innings was made more special because Ganga, Gayle, Morton and Wavell Hinds were all out by the 14th over with only 61 on the board.

By the time the Hooper-Chanderpaul partnership stand was finally broken in the 45th over, the pair put together a West Indian fifth-wicket ODI record stand of 154. The previous best was 152 between Viv Richards and Clive Lloyd against Sri Lanka at Brisbane's Wollongabba ground in 1982.

Pakistan skipper Younis was the most successful of the bowlers, claiming two wickets, including Ganga

off the third ball of the match when Rashid Latif held a sharp chance.

Faced with a target of 5.22 runs an over under lights, Pakistan never recovered from the early loss of openers Afridi and Naved Latif. Afridi was caught at square leg off Pedro Collins in the second over and Naved Latif fell in the third, trapped leg-before by Mervyn Dillon.

There was a lot of fury in the way the West Indies demolished the Pakistani batting line-up. Pickings had been lean for the Windies in Sharjah - until today. Half the Pakistani side were eligible for showers by the 23rd over when only 86 runs were on the board. Shoaib Malik, who hit that fine unbeaten century in the previous match, made 37 when he was sixth out, bowled by a Hooper off-break, to make it six for 91.

What a difference a game or two makes. Inzamam ul-Haq, who opened in the previous match, was dropped to number seven due to his poor form. Inzamam looked to be recapturing some of his attractive, enterprising strokes when he was bowled for 27, trying to play a reverse sweep off part-time spinner Gayle. Gayle also took the last three wickets, including Rashid Latif for 37, to finish with a career-best four for 19.

Predictably, Hooper won the man-of-the-match award while Abdur Razzaq took the man-of-the-series honours.

CHAPTER 39

PROBE

Many noteworthy achievements in cricket in the past two years have been overshadowed by the match-fixing scandal.

The international game's credibility was torpedoed by a series of incidents, particularly the life ban on the tragic South African captain Hansie Cronje after his forced admission that he took money from a bookmaker. There was a life ban on another Test skipper, Mohammad Azharuddin, for match-fixing, while Saleem Malik, the former captain of Pakistan has also been ousted for life.

Sharjah, as everywhere, has struggled to absorb the steady drip of extraordinary revelations, allegations and incidents. With this in mind, Clive Lloyd, the former West Indies captain, headed a three-man panel investigating match-fixing and betting allegations against those involved in organising international cricket in Sharjah.

CBFS chairman Abdulrahman Bukhatir himself ordered the inquiry following reports that some matches were allegedly fixed. "We know we are clean," said Bukhatir. "We want to set the record straight and that's why we want an independent panel to look into the charges."

The panel included an ex-Sharjah police offer and a legal expert from Britain, according to Bukhatir. The CBFS was "determined", said Bukhatir, to "supplement the ICC and other cricket boards' efforts aimed at cleaning the image of the game."

Sunil Gavaskar and Ian Botham were appointed with broad briefs to keep an eye on the integrity of the game in Sharjah. Sharjah and its officialdom went from

Ian Botham... impeccable

strength to strength. Sharjah received Test match status and a concept similar to the UAE offshore experiment is being launched in Morocco, totally set up by Bukhatir machine. It is being headed by Stephen Comacho, former West Indies opening batsman who later became secretary of the West Indies Cricket Board.

Despite recent upheavals, cricket continues to hold its traditional pre-eminence among summer sports, particularly on the subcontinent, where about 40 per cent of all Tests and 30 per cent of one-day internationals are played. Names such as Nazir, Stewart and Singh are likely to serve the sport with distinction. The newcomers hit the ball hard and often, and their destinies appear exciting.

Over the last century, player quality and team success has historically gone in cycles. Such has been the case in Sharjah in these short 20 years with the seemingly unbeatable West Indies being reduced to also-rans. There are few immediate signs that the decline can be arrested, but some youngsters playing cricket on a beach somewhere in the Caribbean will have something to say about that. The glory days of Worrell, Weekes, Hall, Holding, Roberts, Haynes, Richards et al, may be long gone, but the renaissance is not out of reach. It never is.

The upheaval over the Cronje match-fixing affair – Sharjah was the disgraced skipper's last international series – brought Shaun Pollock to the helm of South African cricket. He had been groomed for the position, but would not have expected to receive the honour for quite a few years or under such circumstances.

Since the inception of international cricket at Sharjah the subcontinent has acquired a fourth Test playing country, Bangladesh (early regulars on the Sharjah ODI scene) and a new one from Africa, Zimbabwe. South Africa also returned from the wilderness.

The Australians struggled in Sharjah and pretty much everywhere in the '80s in the early days, but that has certainly changed around the world to the

The tragic Hanse Cronje sits alone at Sharjah during his last international tournament

*Cricket's extraordinary visionary
Abdulrahman Bukhatir*

extent that the current team are known as 'The Dominators'. Gilchrist is tipped to shatter all wicket-keeper batsmen records. The Australians have adapted to the higher-intensity of the modern game better than anyone - further evidence of the sport going in cycles. And what a moment it will be when Brett Lee measures out his run for the first time in Sharjah while Shoaib Akhtar, a Sharjah favourite, paws the ground in the nets. The pair, who briefly played Sydney grade cricket for the Mosman club, are keen to settle the issue of who is fastest.

For all the new sophisticated coaching and technology, the cornerstone of cricket, in Sharjah and across the spectrum, remains that a match can change at any given moment, the greatest innings can end with one ball. A single stroke can decide a match as did Miandad's last-ball, last-gasp six.

Cricket will always have to fend off a few bouncers as it did with turn-of-the-century player revolts, Bodyline, the WSC 'Circus' and the recent match-fixing scandals, but it will keep demonstrating the highest levels of adaptability and performance under pressure. The game in Sharjah, in such humble surroundings and on a concrete wicket, will continue to expand, intrigue and please.

Old fast bowlers never die - they just shorten their run-ups. And cricket's road goes on forever . . .

Shaun Pollock... took over during a crisis

The future... Ricky Ponting, Australia's dashing new limited-overs captain

CHAPTER 40

CBFS BENEFICIARIES 1981-2001

1981
Hanif Mohammed
Asif Iqbal
Madhav Mantri

1982
Sunil Gavaskar
Intikhab Alam
Nazar Mohammed
S Gupta

Sunil Gavaskar

1983
Gundappa Vishwanath
Zaheer Abbas
Alim-ud-Din
Ramakant Desai

Zaheer Abbas

1984
Bishen Bedi
Imran Khan
Salim Durani

Imran Khan

1985 (March)
Wasim Bari
Syed Kirmani
Gul Mohammed
Eknath Solkar

1985 (November)
Clive Lloyd
Vijay Merchant
Waqar Hasan

1986 (April)
Dilip Vengsarkar
Javed Miandad
Wazir Mohammed
Vijay Hazare

Dilip Vengsarkar

1986 (December)
Joel Garner

1987
Mudassar Nazar
Kapil Dev
Mushtaq Ali
Mustaq Mohammed

1988 (April)
Lala Amarnath

Kapil Dev

Mohinder Amarnath
Richard Hadlee

1988 (October)
Ravi Shastri
Mohsin Khan
Bhagwat Chandrashekar
Munir Malik

1989 (March)
Abdul Qadir
Salauddin Ahmed

Abdul Qadir

1989 (October)
Iqbal Qasim
Vivian Richards
Pahlan 'Polly' Umrigar
Fazal Mehmood
K. Srikanth

1990 (May)
Ghulam Ahmed
Saleem Malik
Imtiaz Ahmed
Madan Lal
Allan Border
Duleep Mendis

Allan Border

Michael Holding

1990 (December)
Wallis Mathias
Tauseef Ahmed

1991 (October)
Gordon Greenidge
Cottari Nayadu
Erapally Prasanna
Mahood Hussein
Wasim Raja

1993 (February)
Rameez Raja
Sikander Bakht

1993 (November)
Desmond Haynes
Shoaib Mohammed
Mohammed Nazir

1994 (April)
Rusi Modi
Srinivasarraghavan
Venkatraghavan
Mohammed Azharuddin
Pervez Sajjad
Haroon Rashid
Salim Yousef

1995 (October)
Javed Burki
Naushad Ali
Abdul Hafiz Kardar
Michael Holding
Abu Fuard
A. Saadat

1996 (April)
Chetan Chauhan
Yashpal Sharma
Hemu Adhikari
Shafqat Rana
Naseemul Ghani
Wasim Akram
M.E.Z. Ghazali

1996 (November)
Sadiq Mohammed
Talat Ali
Ijaz Ahmed

1997 (April)
Waqar Younis
Saeed Ahmed
Zulfiqar Ali Ahmed
Haji Israr Bhattee
M. Aslam Khokhar
Ghulam Mustafa Khan

1997 (December)
Ashok Vinoo Mankad
Dilip Rasiklal Doshi
Gulabrai Ramchand
Mohammed Asif Mujtaba
Saleem Altaf
Richie Richardson

1998 (April)
B Parsuram Patel
S Nandalal Yadav
P Khirod Ray
Talat Ali
Javed Akhtar

1998 (November)
Roger Binny
Aush Gaekwad
Narendra Naren Tamhane

1999 (April)
Narimam Contractor
Karsan Ghavri
Aaqib Javed
Khan Mohammed
Sandeep Patil
Malcolm Marshall
Mushtaq Ahmed
Aamer Malik

2000 (April)
Chandu Borde
Bapu Nadkarni
Moin Khan
Saeed Anwar

Saeed Anwar

2000 (Oct)
Navjot Singh Sidhu
Rusi Surti

2001 (Oct-Nov)
Mansoor Akhtar
Mohammed Ilyas
Younis Ahmed
Aftab Baluch
Liaquat Ali
Afgha Zahid
Azmat Rana

CHAPTER 41

IN FACT...

Sharjah Ground Records

Highest team total

338-4 (50 overs):
New Zealand v Bangladesh (1990)
333-7 (50 overs):
West Indies v Sri Lanka (1995)
332-3 (50 overs):
Australia v Sri Lanka (1990)

Lowest team total

54 (26.3 overs):
Sri Lanka v West Indies (2000)
55 (28.3 overs):
Sri Lanka v West Indies (1986)
64 (35.5 overs):
New Zealand v Sri Lanka (1986)

Highest individual innings (Sharjah)

*189 Sanath Jayasuriya
Sri Lanka v India (2000)
169 Brian Lara
West Indies v Sri Lanka (1995)
153 Brian Lara
West Indies v Pakistan (1995)

Sanath Jayasuriya

Highest individual scores (worldwide)

194 Saeed Anwar
Pakistan v India
Independence Cup, Chidambaram
Stadium,Chennai (1997)
189* Vivian Richards
West Indies v England
Old Trafford, Manchester (1984)
189 Sanath Jayasuriya
Champions Trophy
Sharjah CA Stadium (2000)

Fastest 150

Brian Lara : (111 balls)
West Indies v Sri Lanka (1993)

Fastest 100

Basit Ali: (67 balls)
Pakistan v West Indies (1993)

Fastest 50
Simon O'Donnell: (18 balls)
Australia v Sri Lanka (1990)

*Simon
O'Donnell*

Best bowling

*7-30: Muttiah Muralitharan
Sri Lanka v India
(2000) (world record)
7-37: Aquib Javed
Pakistan v India (1991)

6-14: Imran Khan
Pakistan v India 1985
6-26: Waqar Younis
Pakistan v Sri Lanka (1990)

*Muttiah
Muralitharan*

Record batting partnerships

(1st wicket) 204:
Saeed Anwar/Rameez Raja
Pakistan v Sri Lanka (1993)
(2nd) 263
Aamer Sohail/Inzamam ul-Haq
Pakistan v New Zealand (1994)
(3rd) 226
Marvan Atapattu/Mahela
Jayaawardene
Sri Lanka v India (2000)
(4th) 172
Saleem Malik/ Basit Ali
Pakistan v West Indies (1993)
(5th) 166
Sanath Jayasuriya/Russell Arnold
Sri Lanka v India (2000)
(6th) 154
Richie Richardson/Jeff Dujon
West Indies v Pakistan (1991)
(7th) 115
Adam Parore/Lee Germon
New Zealand v Pakistan (1996)
(8th) 81*

Saleem Malik/Aquib Javed
Pakistan v South Africa (1996)
(9th) 45
Richie Richardson/Ian Bishop
West Indies v Pakistan (1991)
(10th) 29
Carlisle Best/CourtneyWalsh
West Indies v Pakistan (1989)

CourtneyWalsh

Most dismissals in an innings by a wicketkeeper

5 (3ct 2st) Kiran More:
India v New Zealand - (1988)
5 (5ct) Hashan Tillekeratne:
Sri Lanka v Pakistan - (1990)
5 (4 ct 1st)
Romesh Kaluwitharrana:
Sri Lanka v Pakistan (1995)

Test records Sharjah

Centurians

Rashid Latif 150
(First Test Pakistan v West Indies
2002)

Yousuf Youhana 146
(First Test Pakistan v West Indies
2002)

Yousuf Youhana

Record partnerships

204 (sixth wicket stand)
Yousuf Youhana – Rashid Latif
(First Test Pakistan v West Indies
2002)

Best bowling

Shoaib Akhtar five for 24
(First Test Pakistan v West Indies
2002)

Best batting

150 Younis Khan
(2nd Test Pakistan v West Indies)

Rashid Latif

Sachin Tendulkar